ACKNOWLEDGMENTS

To Sharon, my wife and life partner, who supported me in all our real estate ventures with her invaluable insight and suggestions.

To my children, Brian and Melanie, who were my able assistants around the buildings as they were growing up and continue to inspire me every day.

To Vida for her outstanding help with editing this manuscript, its book design and other great suggestions in its publication.

INTRODUCTION

Most books on managing residential property are one part truth, one part fiction and one part mechanical. They miss the most important point... **the most important ingredient in successfully managing your properties -** *the residents*.

Some books take an antiseptic approach to the task of managing the buildings. A data-driven approach maxes out the numbers and forgets that those numbers are in constant flux - even with a fixed rate mortgage on the property.

This book on property management is different because it focuses on a new bottom line - which in short, is your success and sanity. It is a strategy that focuses on not only making a decent return on your investment; but just as importantly, on customer satisfaction - thus eliminating 90% of the problems you might encounter in managing residential property.

This guide is not about flipping apartments or swapping apartment contracts. It's not about generating 'mailbox money' without any active involvement on your part. It's not about wholesaling properties and collecting an 'assignment fee.'

This is a quick-start guide to finding, analyzing, managing, improving, and profiting from rental properties. It provides common sense and real world strategies that actually work. I will not offer any 'streetwise' strategies that infer one can get something for nothing with little to no effort and make a huge profit in doing so.

Based on my thirty years of real world experience in the business of buying, managing, and improving apartment properties; I will show you how to master successful habits that then become routine in your own management style.

There are no absolute guarantees of success and this guide may not be the final answer to every question about real estate investing a newcomer to the field might have. However, if you follow the practical principles outlined here, you will find yourself on the road to success. It won't be a cakewalk - but then again, nothing worthwhile ever comes without effort.

The future for owning and managing small apartment buildings is great and getting better ... if you know what you're doing.

> **From My Perspective**
>
> Sprinkled throughout this guide are personal antidotes and life stories that can be invaluable lessons for anyone new to real estate ownership and managing residential property. These personal stories will be shown in boxes like this for your visual convenience.

This book is about more than just mindset. The right mindset is essential in dealing with management issues and other problems associated with owning property. Also important is the right kind of discipline; a process and a strategy to be able to manage apartment buildings with a minimum of problems; both tenant problems and mechanical issues.

You will learn a few simple steps to make your role as property owner easier and more profitable. It's all about organizing your management skills to get the most benefit with the least amount of stress. It's about unlocking your potential to influence and engage others to help you reach that goal.

It's about using your emotional intelligence as well as financial and managerial intelligence to best utilize your own strategic set of guidelines for managing your properties. You want to become an effective manager of buildings so that you can harness the power of thinking without thinking about it. Your pattern of success will then become a regimen you follow automatically. By doing so you will avoid critical mistakes that can be costly to your bottom line and might drive residents away

It's all about working smarter - not harder or longer. It's about using data to help you process information and create sustainability for energy usage in each property. It's about making the most of your time and being productive with the tools you will learn to use in this guide.

I hope this guide will help you avoid the same mistakes I made as I began in the business.

Good Luck,

Denis J. LaComb

CONTENTS

Acknowledgments	iii
Introduction	v
Approach to Real Estate Investing	1
Property Selection	15
Attracting Quality Residents	27
Tenant Selection: The Key Ingredient to Success	35
Financials & Recordkeeping	69
Property Maintenance	81
Future Prosperity & Growth	101
Glossary	105
About the Author	119

APPROACH TO REAL ESTATE INVESTING

Investing in small apartments requires a concentrated study of this aspect of the business. As Warren Buffet has been quoted saying many times: "Stick with what you know and focus on the long term." It means understanding this segment of the real estate business as well as anyone else. Small apartments are a business entity whose profit picture for decades has been reasonably predictable. Even as interest rates vary and financial markets shift and change, the financial basics of managing small apartments have stayed pretty much the same.

Every property has its own list of potential problem areas. This guide will provide you with a strategy to deal with any and all of them. You will be encouraged to keep detailed records to correctly assess the most logical 'next step' when issues arise. The idea here is to be proactive instead of reactive. You need to prepare for, anticipate, and know the logical steps to take when dealing with any issue.

At the risk of sounding redundant, let me repeat that this is not a get rich quick scheme. There are no surefire recipes or formulas to follow here for guaranteed success. Rather it is a slow and steady routine with as little pain as possible. If you are looking for a quick fix or easy money, keep watching so-called reality TV but forget about the reality part. You probably will not succeed to any measurable degree and you most certainly will encounter a lot of frustration along the way.

If you are willing to work methodically through these principles, if you experiment and find the right strategy that works for you (one that matches your personality, your patience and your own particular lifestyle) then your chances of success are increased exponentially. Remember there are few guarantees in life but this book will take you a long way toward achieving your goal of successful apartment management.

It is not enough just to imagine yourself as a landlord or property owner, you must own that vision. You do that by taking the actions necessary to make your dreams, your visions, and your self-image come true. Simply stated, you must be willing to put in the work necessary to achieve your real estate goals.

Study the real estate business relative to your specific interest…in this case, managing small apartment buildings. Educate yourself on the latest trends and developments in the marketplace. Continue to network with other professionals in the field. Develop a strategy for success and then follow through on that plan.

You must decide if this is rental property, investment property, or someone's *home*. The moniker is very important because it defines what business you are in. Rental property connotes maximizing rents. Investment property connotes a total concentration on the bottom line often at the exclusion of those entities that will help you get there.

Why has real estate historically been a good investment but hardly a no-brainer?

Real estate investments have historically been a good investment as long as certain principles are followed. Unlike most other investments, real estate can provide a steady source of income, debt reduction, equity build-up, appreciation, tax benefits, and leverage.

Down through the ages in this country and abroad, the individuals and families that made their mark through real estate among other investments are legendary. Storied names like Rockefeller, Hearst, Mellon, Carnegie, Roosevelt, and Kennedy. The list continues today with Trump, Zeller, Turner, Emerson, Singleton, Malone, Kelley and Irving.

By the latest estimation, over a third of the world's wealth is tied up in real estate. Even if they made their initial fortune in other investments most of these millionaires and billionaires protect their investments at least in part through real estate holdings.

There is a caveat. Unlike stock purchases and some other investment vehicles, one should not buy real estate and then wait for something positive to happen. To be successful the buyer must make things happen. That is why knowledge is critical to success in this business. The old paradigm rules here: The more you know about the business; the better equipped you will be to make good business decisions.

First out of the gate, proper financing is one key component to success. If you find yourself behind the financial eight ball right from the start, then any future success will be tempered by those past financial constraints. Along with financing, proper valuation is another key component to success.

You only get there if you've been able to realistically value the property in the first place. A study of economic supply and demand trends will help you appreciate and understand the needs of the seller against and with your own desire to purchase. Remember, it must be done on a local level. Valuations and real estate trends can vary from region to region, state to state, county to county - and even neighborhood to neighborhood. Thus, any talk of housing trends and changes must be put into the proper perspective.

With the exception of a powerful outside force such as a sudden and extreme increase in interest rates; all real estate is, in fact, local. Each property must be analyzed within its geographical location, type of investment, investor, and capital structure relative to its location.

Location and timing play into this equation. Just as location plays a key role in evaluating a property, so too does timing. The old adage is never out of style: "buy low and sell high." That can also be a real plus if your property is properly priced, but offers unique opportunities for future improvements, and thus price appreciation. Timing is also important in terms of the availability of money to invest and the terms associated with that transaction.

Your own analysis of local real estate trends must focus on your specific area of interest. If your interest lies with small apartment buildings, then while other trends such as sales of single family homes might indirectly influence your own real estate category; your focus should still be on apartment buildings and little else. Any market research must include location, market rents, and demand for units.

There is always a natural conflict between the values placed on a property by its owner verses the value placed on it by the potential buyer. Replacement values placed on the property by insurance companies only tell part of the story of true value as do property tax valuations. In the end, the appraised value placed on the property by a real estate appraiser will probably get you the closest to the true value of the property. Comps also count since buyers always look to see what other similar buildings in that neighborhood recently sold for.

This is not because of the intrinsic pluses or minuses of the property itself, but rather what other similar properties in that neighborhood are selling for - today. In almost every single case, the comp value is the only value that gets the most attention from buyers and sellers alike.

Sellers usually see a high value for their property and the buyer usually thinks it should be less. In the end, the market determines the current value. This is not yesterday's value or what it might garner in the near future, but what it would sell for today.

What is in store for the next five years?
…is the wrong question to ask!

I sure as heck don't have a crystal ball - but if you look at the past, it will give you a good indication of what to expect in the future. Historically, real estate has proven itself a solid investment. Through its tax benefits, depreciation and appreciation, well managed real estate can provide attractive returns to its owners.

The challenge here is to get past the hype and hyperbole and try to assess an accurate picture of real estate at the time you intend to invest in it. It does not really help your quest to watch real estate television or listen to alleged real estate gurus selling their version of some 'get rich quick' scheme.

Instead of trying to guess which direction real estate might take in the near future, it makes more sense to know exactly what your own goals are relative to purchasing real estate *now*.

Your goals should not, repeat *not*, simply focus on how much money you hope to make in the transaction. Instead, you should concentrate on an honest self-evaluation of yourself as a real estate investor.

SELF EVALUATION QUESTIONNAIRE

Are you comfortable with a large mortgage?

Are you willing to take risks?

Are you cautious when it comes to money management or money issues?

Is your wife, husband, or partner cautious with money?

Does your partner share the same financial goals as you?

Will your partner be a part of any real estate transaction or will they be sitting on the sidelines?

How much time do you want to spend investing in real estate?

Is real estate investing a full-time job, part-time job, or a sideline for weekends and a few evenings a week?

How long do you envision owning this property?

Is this something you would like to do far into the future or within a short time frame until you have retired or moved ahead in your real job?

Are you a people person?

Do you like to negotiate?

How well do you handle conflict?

I never realized it until I got into the business that I love the idea of adding value to any property I purchased. After a while, I made it a point to look for undiscovered potential that might add some degree of value to any purchase I made. I was constantly looking for ways to keep my current residents happy and make the property attractive to potential renters in the future.

Updating or remodeling the individual units would bring higher rents and a better quality of resident. Adding a washer and dryer would add income. Garages would add income. Other amenities might add income or make the property more attractive to potential renters.

I am not a technology person, but I do know that new technologies have affected the creation, maintenance, and refurbishment of homes and commercial buildings in a myriad of ways. There are now apps for almost any and every application imaginable. They have become a part of the modern culture landscape. You cannot afford not to know what apps might be available to help you in managing your properties.

[More on this in the Maintenance and Upkeep Section.]

Along with examining your goals and objectives pursuant to real estate, you should have a solid business plan. Not only should your business plan cover the financial aspects of your purchase, it should also address other issues such as whether it is going to be a short-term or long-term investment? Who is going to manage the property? What are the projected costs for refurbishment of the property, adding value wherever possible, maintenance and upkeep, and associated taxes?

"This time it's different"
(NO, *it's not!*)

Forget the pundits. Whether they are pontificating about the latest and greatest in real estate investments or warning the world that the housing market is falling, they are probably wrong. They were wrong before…many times. They will be wrong again.

In the early 2000s, the hottest trend around was fractional ownership of large resort properties especially in Mexico and on the west coast. Then hotel condominiums became a hot item. It seemed as if everyone was buying second homes or vacation properties and renting them out as every month they gained more value in appreciation. That was before 2004, and then again before 2008.

Cable TV carried several series about flipping properties for huge profits. No-money-down get rich quick schemes flooded the networks. Foreclosures were made to look attractive and a no-brainer for even the novice real estate investor. REITs were a sure thing.

If that wasn't enough to lure even the most timid, there were infomercials on how to make huge profits out of discounted paper, real estate options, real estate contracts, bank owned properties, government tax liens and other financial products that all seemed too good to be true.

For most of these investment schemes, the time to make a real profit had long since passed before they were offered up to the general public. It was the time of the new dot-coms and the new economy. Now it's the green economy, alternative energies, and even crowdfunding.

Certainly, these schemes have been executed and will continue to be hatched in this country and around the world. Nevertheless, I would suggest that it takes a very savvy and experienced wheeler-dealer to pull off those schemes. It is not for the faint of heart or the inexperienced. You and I probably couldn't do it in a million years. What is that old adage ... if it sounds too good to be true...?

Some real estate guides promise to help you build a system so that you do not have to do any work yourself. Think about it! No system runs entirely on its own unless, of course, it is something like a lawn sprinkler system and even that needs to be tended to each spring and fall. Nothing is one hundred percent failsafe. There are no automatic apartment systems that will entirely relieve you of your responsibility as a landlord and property manager.

It takes work to succeed in this business. It can be a lot of hard work until you have your strategies in place. And while it's true that you must be agile and ready to adapt in today's changing market conditions, the basic principles of managing properties have always remained the same.

The only person who profits from marketing such nonsense is the huckster selling it. The only one losing is the sap buying it. Generally, what is passed off as 'get rich quick' is total bullshit.

Multiply your chances of success by learning how to attract and retain satisfied residents who want to live in your units and who care about your building as much as you do. These residents will become your eyes and ears in your absence.

It takes disciplined entrepreneurship to build and grow a business. That happens through the proper execution of management strategies that really work. You will be building a business to last while adding value to your holdings. You will learn to avoid making costly mistakes while waking up your creative potential. Your goal and my wish for you are to grow rich slowly and still have a satisfying life in the process.

In today's fast-paced world of competitive workplaces and turbulent economic conditions, we need tools to manage rental properties and other people's lives. The old style landlord who simply collected rent and did little else is a relic of the past. If you want your properties to grow in value and your business to succeed then you have to approach your role as landlord differently.

Don't be misguided by the newest series on TV that shows you how some newbie stumbled into real estate and made a fortune despite themselves. It makes for great television viewing, but it's hardly based on reality. Forget the newest real estate products and schemes. Stick with the tried and true that has proven itself over the decades.

The only seismic shift that has occurred over the last couple of years has been the proliferation of apartment complexes. We are well past 2008 when no one could sell their condominiums or single-family homes and thus were renting them out to anyone who could make their mortgage payment for them.

Gradually, that glut of rental properties on the market shrank and demand began to grow again. Large companies began accumulating or building larger and larger apartment complexes. Technology and sustainable design were added to the mix. This time it is the millennials interested in renting their new homes instead of buying them.

Chapter Summary:
Down through the ages real estate has been a proven investment vehicle. It offers unique advantages that other investments do not offer. Real estate fads come and go; but if managed with a focus on renter selection and the bottom line, owning small apartment buildings can bring solid results.

PROPERTY SELECTION

This section focuses on selecting small apartment buildings as a long-term investment strategy. Owning and managing small apartment buildings can be an excellent way to enter into this business and get started before venturing into other real estate fields if you so desire.

The Property Itself
The real estate agent puffed up his chest and proudly proclaimed to me that it was just as easy to manage a large apartment building as it was a small one. He may not have been your typical real estate agent but he was still full of it. There are enough of them out there that you had better educate yourself about the property before you start believing what any agent tells you about it.

Before buying any property you must ask yourself some hard questions right up front.

It can't be an emotional issue or one that isn't approached with honest self-evaluation. Forget all the platitudes the agent will probably heap on you about your ability to become a great landlord. Only you know your own strengths and weaknesses, not some salesman.

I am an introvert. I have to 'work' at dealing with other individuals. I am not comfortable in confrontational situations or ones that create a boss-employee environment. I understood that going into apartment management, but I was willing to give it a chance. I didn't go into it blindly. I knew just where my own comfort level lay and I wasn't about to cross over the line of demarcation just to satisfy someone else's inflated ego.

Managing a five unit building was just the right size for my personality. After a year or so, I felt I could add to that with another building and another five units. I found that I liked four and five unit buildings. They were more manageable. The size per unit was usually much larger than a building with more than four or five units. I could charge more per unit and I had fewer folks per building to deal with. It was the perfect fit for me and my personality.

What is a good fit for you?
Perhaps a single family home or duplex is right for you. I was never interested in a single family home or duplex because I felt they were as much work with less cash return than a larger building. Your feelings may be different from mine.

My prejudice was deeply ingrained on the kinds of properties I wanted to buy. I saw little difference between a four or five unit building. Once you start looking at an eight or ten unit building, the issues start to multiply exponentially. For my money, a fourplex or fiveplex building was the way to start. If you want to expand with more buildings or larger buildings after you've gotten your hands dirty and some months or years under your belt, you'll be in a much better position to decide just where you want to go next.

Your best bet is almost always a solid building owned by an

experienced owner for more than several years. Anything different makes the building or the owner suspect. As a newbie in this business, I would never recommend that you buy a property from a bank, a HUD house, a vacant house, one in foreclosure or auction, a fire-damaged house or a handyman special. Perhaps after you've been in the business for a while and have earned your real estate chops you might venture into those minefields.

The location of your rental property
As much as I hate that real estate moniker that is bantered about so frequently about 'location, *location*, **location**' - it really is true that the location of your property can make all the difference in the world in terms of your success.

Study after study by cities, metropolitan councils, and planning agencies all point to the same general amenities that attract solid reliable residents. These include safe neighborhoods, high quality parks and recreation facilities, a myriad of arts, culture, and nightlife. In addition, nearby shopping and entertainment venues such as coffee shops are a huge plus.

The reality is that you won't find many of those amenities in a sketchy part of town. It's really as simple as that. I never cease to be amazed at the yahoos who buy a piece of property in a bad part of town and then complain about the kind of folks they're attracting as renters. What did they expect? Never buy in a sketchy neighborhood…period.

If you don't know about the neighborhood ahead of time, then find out before you go snooping around for properties to purchase. It's all about personal safety for you, your family, and your residents. Personal safety should be your # 1 priority. Understand that crimes can happen anywhere, at any time ... but by all means, put the odds in your favor right from the start.

My buildings were in a great neighborhood but it was still the big city. Over a thirty-year period various neighbors around us experienced car break-ins, window-peepers, bikes taken off back porches, break-ins into the basement to steal laundry coins, etc. All you can do is make sure your buildings are in a good neighborhood, have a secured building, and good residents. After that, you can only trust fate and good luck to keep danger away from your front door.

You know when you're in a good part of town. You don't have to rely on crime statistics and employment records. Just by driving through the neighborhoods, you can tell if the homes are clean and well maintained. Is the area quiet relative to local traffic and congestion? Is there plenty of off-street parking for multi-family buildings? Are there a lot of amenities within walking distance from most homes?

Don't buy on a busy street
Would you want to live on a busy street? Neither would your residents. While it may be good for visibility, it doesn't add to the peace and quiet that you want for your residents.

I had two corner buildings. One was on a busy street and the other was a block away on a quiet side street. Guess which one was more preferable for new prospective residents?

While I didn't get as many eyeballs for my signs in front on the quiet street, it still presented very nice curb appeal.

Tax-wise, both buildings cost me more money because I was on the corner and thus paid per foot in front of the building as well as along the side of the building. I also didn't have neighbors on one side of either building so that was attractive in another sense.

Several of my buildings were within walking distance of nearby colleges. That being said, I would never buy a building closer than a half mile to any college campus. I wasn't interested in renting to students (generally speaking) and the threat of parties nearby on weekends was enough to keep me a proper distance away.

Remember it is the job of any real estate agent to sell the property. Therefore, any amenity in the building or nearby is seen by them as a plus or benefit to you the buyer. In reality, some amenities are good and some can be a pain. It's important to differentiate between the two.

GOOD AMENITIES

- ### **Garages**

Garages are golden. Not only can they provide extra income, they're a great added benefit to your unit even if you don't charge for their use. Make sure your lease agreement clearly states the rules governing use of the garage. If in the rare instance that a resident doesn't use the garage, you can always make additional income by renting it out to someone else.

- ### **Laundry facilities**

Another top amenity is laundry facilities. Most are located in the basement of a building. Based on comments made by potential residents, it is critical that the laundry room area be well lit and very clean. No one, especially women, wants to venture into the basement at night if it isn't well lit, clean, and secure.

I had an outside company manage my washer and dryer in one building and I got a cut of their revenues. If there was a mechanical problem, it was their responsibility to fix it promptly. If they didn't respond promptly I would threaten to get another service and that usually got it fixed ASAP.

If your building comes with its own washer and dryer and you get to keep all the revenues, that's all the better.

Remember to make sure that area is secure. Primarily, make sure your back door to the building is always locked. I had other buildings in my neighborhood broken into because their back doors weren't always secure.

♦ **Sunrooms**

In Minnesota, a sunroom facing in any direction is a natural plus. Some folks use it for a quiet reading spot, an office, or a plant sanctuary. It doesn't really matter how that space is utilized, in any cold climate it is a wonderful respite from the cold outside.

The only caveat here is to make sure it doesn't become a third bedroom. The city will probably frown on such use and you don't need the hassle of an additional roommate to muck up the relationship of the pair already there.

♦ **Wi-Fi – Cable**

If it's available and you can afford it, I've always found that cable and Wi-Fi as part of the lease package are an extremely attractive benefit to your residents. It certainly is justification for higher rents than your neighbors who don't offer such amenities.

♦ **Storage units**

Most older buildings have storage units in the basement. It really is a must for most folks who always seem to have extra things they haul around from one building to the next.

♦ Washer/Dryers in the units

Most older buildings don't have washers and dryers in the unit themselves. It's a plus if they do, but a nice setup in the basement is often just as good.

♦ Decks or porches in front or back of building

Decks or porches that are *structurally* a part of the building's design are attractive. Add-on structures can be a source of real concern for owners and insurance companies alike. You will notice I mention this type in the 'Bad Amenities' list.

♦ Nice landscaping

Nice curb appeal goes far beyond simply the visual attractiveness of your building and its close surroundings. Instead, it speaks volumes about the building's owner and its occupants. Great curb appeal tells any prospective renter that your building is probably very attractive inside as well as outside. It hints at appreciative residents and their pride in the place they call home.

♦ Gardening

There was always a garden plot behind my buildings and free gardening tools to use. Some of the residents made use of it while others weren't at all interested. It didn't matter if it was used from one year to the next. The fact is it was there to be used if anyone so desired.

It also sent a message that I cared about the environment and the overall appeal of my building. On many occasions, the garden quickly became another one of those small amenities that residents came to enjoy and appreciate. It became a natural gathering spot for folks on weekends and became the envy of many of our neighbors.

♦ Safe and quiet neighborhoods

One of my overriding concerns in selecting a building to purchase was the simple question: would I want to live in that neighborhood myself? I never cease to be amazed at property owners who buy in bad neighborhoods and then are surprised when they attract questionable residents. Why would they expect top quality residents in a third tier neighborhood?

It became paramount to seek out buildings in neighborhoods that I considered safe. On many weekends, I would bring my kids to the buildings as I worked there. My son would cut the grass and my daughter would run around the building and do chores for me. If I thought for a second that they weren't in a safe environment, I would never have bought that building in the first place.

I also wanted buildings where my wife might venture at night if an emergency arose and I couldn't deal with it. The personal safety of my wife and kids was always considered in any purchase of my rental property.

♦ Nearby facilities

It is always a huge plus to have facilities nearby that residents can use on a daily or weekly basis. My buildings were always close to grocery stores, restaurants, shops, and entertainment venues.

BAD AMENITIES

While the name 'bad amenities' might seem like an oxymoron, it really isn't. There are features in any building that might seem attractive on the surface but in reality can be a real pain in the backside.

♦ Three bedroom units

All of my buildings were built in the 1920s and 1930s. As such, they came with sunrooms in front of each unit. As mentioned before, I made it a notation on the lease that the sun room was to remain just that and never to be turned into a third bedroom. That wasn't negotiable; it was one of the terms for staying in the unit.

I had numerous opportunities to buy buildings that had one or more three-bedroom units in them. For me it was a deal breaker. I just walked away each time.

Three roommates are a world apart from just two. In my experience in the business for over thirty years and in talking with other landlords, I've found that three roommates have the potential to be a real pain. If problems don't arise almost immediately, they usually will over the long term.

What tends to happen, is that two of the three become close and the third is left out of the equation. That third party then wants to leave and someone else will want to take his or her place. It doesn't matter how often the third party is replaced, there will always be a schism between an individual and a pair that naturally forms.

♦ Fireplaces

While they may seem an attractive feature to any unit, the reality is that they are both dangerous and a major liability for you and the occupant of that unit. In fact, they are a major headache with insurance companies and residents alike. I have yet to have heard of any unit with a fireplace that didn't invite some kind of problem or issue.

Avoid them at all costs unless they are simply decorative

and not functioning.

♦ Add-on decks or porches

Decks or porches that are not *structurally* a part of the building's design can be a major concern for owner and insurance companies.

Almost every summer, there are reports of over-crowding on a deck or porch and its subsequent collapse. It doesn't matter what your lease says about the maximum number of people on that porch or deck. Nor does it matter what a sign out there says as to the maximum number of bodies allowed. If the party is going well, people will naturally gravitate outdoors onto a porch or deck.

I've heard of building owners who removed porches and decks rather than face the consequences of a collapse and the lawsuits that are certain to follow. This is a classic case of buyer beware!

♦ Hustle and bustle

There is a major difference between visiting a neighborhood that is bustling with activity and living in that same area. One is fun to visit because you're doing just that - visiting. If you lived there, you would probably want a much quieter neighborhood. So would any potential resident looking to rent from you.

Nearby student housing, a campus, or a commercial business strip is going to attract traffic; both human and vehicular at all times of the day and night. It is not conducive to quiet living, which is what you should be selling anyone looking to rent from you.

If your prospective resident is looking for a place close to the action, then they are not the kind of resident that you should be attracting.

What adds value to your building?
By studying both the good amenities and the bad ones, you should have a good idea of what you're looking for in a building to purchase. Some are obvious such as garages, laundry facilities, sunrooms, Wi-Fi, cable, storage space for each unit, and landscaping.

There are some other often forgotten amenities that also add value if only in a subtle way. For example, a clean and well-lit entry way or lobby. Secure mailboxes and a place for larger items such as magazines and large envelopes. Secured doors in front and in back of the building. Motion sensitive lights outside. Large trash receptacles are a must. A spot for a garden in back.

Finally, location is paramount. I always tried to buy a building in a residential neighborhood. I wanted to get as residential as possible because this fit the type of people I wanted to attract to my building and neighborhood.

Chapter Summary:
As important as tenant selection will eventually be, the purchase of the right property ranks just as high. There are good amenities and bad amenities to consider. There should also be value added elements present in any building you consider purchasing.

DENIS J. LACOMB

ATTRACTING QUALITY ~~TENANTS~~ RESIDENTS

To be truly successful you must make your apartment an attractive home for your residents. If you do not, you could find yourself behind the eight ball in more ways than you want to count.

Even after thirty years in the business, I never owned rental property. I owned apartment buildings, single-family homes, and resort property where people lived. They were proud of their homes and I was proud to be providing that housing stock for them to live in. It was a mutually exclusive arrangement. I did not have tenants in my buildings. I had *residents*. Personally, I think the words 'tenant' and 'renter' almost sound like a kind of slavery.

Attract Your Perfect Residents
A quick glance of any apartment rental guide will show you the high expectations today's renters have for their homes. City properties especially highlight each building's unique characteristic. Study these ads to understand just what your potential residents are looking for in their new homes.

hardwood floors	**on bus line**
built-in buffet	**near transit station**
utilities included	**near bike-share**
heat, water, and	**cable/internet ready**
waste removal paid	**free wifi**
smoke-free	**balcony**
pet friendly	**storage units available**
contemporary	**bike storage**
brownstone	**newly remodeled**
high ceilings	**updated amenities**
new appliances	**stainless steel appliances**

…are some of the many features these new renters have come to expect in new and older properties alike when selecting a rental.

What can you do with the property you have purchased to meet these expectations? Whether it is installing a granite-like countertop instead of the real thing, new appliances verses stainless steel or polished hardwood floors instead of carpeting. Examine what features you can add to remain competitive in the marketplace.

Fortunately, the same management approach that works for large complexes will work ideally for smaller ones too. There are growing expectations among millennials and other ideal-age residents that must be addressed and met if you are going to attract the ideal renter. When the market shifts again and there is an overabundance of properties and fewer renters, the approach you take will continue to attract the right kind of renter for your properties.

Positive Feedback

It didn't take too long for me to figure that I must have been doing something right. The vast majority of potential renters who came to my front door were impressed just as soon as they got out of their cars or walked up the front steps. Many of them would stop in mid-step and look around before continuing on.

I made it a point to listen very carefully to their comments and questions, which usually revealed what they liked about my place. They liked the location, the exterior of the building, the landscaping, and the clean and well-lit lobby. If we went into the basement, they marveled at how well lit that was also. They liked the clean laundry room and where they could hang their clothes outside during the summer months.

All of this occurred before they even stepped inside one of the units for rent. I'm confident that by presenting a complete package on the outside, they were primed to like the unit even before they stepped inside.

ADD VALUE

This business is replete with phrases for every occasion. One of the more common clichés is to buy smart, add value and then sell smart. While it sounds like the old refrain of buy low and sell high it actually encompasses much more.

There are many ways to add value to your building. The more obvious ones usually garner the most attention but it is often the more overlooked that provide the biggest return on effort and investment. Each one is a simple amenity that adds overall value to the living experience in your building and as such encourages your residents to stay for a long time.

- **Cable and Wi-Fi**

Before Wi-Fi, there was cable. I had one of the first buildings on my block to offer cable to all my residents as part of their rental package. If I were still in business today, it would be both cable and Wi-Fi. Today's renter would expect nothing less.

- **Laundry facilities**

My buildings always had laundry facilities in the basement. Unlike many other older buildings in the neighborhood, my basements were clean, well lit, and secure. Women had no problem going downstairs in the middle of the night. The front and back doors were always secure and the basement had no dark corners in which an intruder might hide.

I seldom raised the cost of the washer and dryer. That became a selling point to prospective renters who knew the cost at regular laundromats down the block. It wasn't a big deal but it was enough to add to the plus side of renting in one of my buildings.

- **Gardening**

There was always a garden plot behind my buildings and free

gardening tools to use.

It really began almost by accident when one of the residents asked if she could start a gardening plot in the back yard to grow lettuce, tomatoes, etc. Once the plot got started, other residents asked to join in the effort.

I simply took extra gardening tools I had at home and left them downstairs for anyone to use, clean up, and return to my gardening bin. The garden quickly became another one of those small amenities that residents came to enjoy and appreciate. No one else on the block with the exception of one single-family house had one like it for years.

♦ **Free exchange**

During one of my purging exercises at home, I ended up with a pile of magazines and books I was going to take to Goodwill. Instead, I took them to the building and left them in the laundry room with a note that anyone was welcome to take any magazine or book there.

It quickly became a swap center for the building. Other residents would leave their old magazines, books, nick-knacks, articles of clothing and other sundry items for others to grab.

If articles were left untouched after a couple of weeks, I would gather them up and then take the load to Goodwill. By getting rid of items that didn't move and continually adding new items, the swap center became a popular spot to check out when folks did their laundry.

♦ **Picnics in the back yard**

I always encouraged my residents to make full use of the backyard for picnics, social gatherings, family events, etc. It simply extended the reach of their living quarters to include the outdoors and enhanced resident harmony within the building.

- ♦ **Green space**

I realized very quickly that the lawns, especially behind my buildings, were very viable and attractive assets to the residents. I did everything I could to encourage them to use that green space as much as they wanted. They always enjoyed the space, the company of their fellow residents, and being outdoors. It also made them more appreciative of being a resident in that particular building.

ADVERTISE VACANCIES

Signs out front
A bright, well-lettered sign in front of your building is mandatory. Don't put it in a window, it won't be seen. The sign should clearly state the number of bedrooms and a number to call...nothing else. I will explain why in the next section on tenant selection.

Craigslist and other social media websites
I was introduced to Craigslist shortly after it began and it was a boon to attracting savvy young professionals who read it before any newspaper ad. I always included very attractive photos of the unit available, number of bedrooms, amenities, rent, lease terms, etc.

I always used their return site for replies and never my own web site or e-mail address. It was safe, secure and afforded me a good number of prospective renters that fit the category I was seeking to fill the unit. Of course, there were occasionally the crazy ones out there, but you could usually see through them quickly.

Craigslist is just one of several social media web sites that now highlight apartments, duplexes, houses, and rooms for rent. These sites are very effective in attracting savvy renters who read them before any newspaper ad. It is imperative that any listing include very attractive photos of the unit available, number of bedrooms, amenities, rent, lease terms, etc. Posting absolutely all of the information clearly available saves you time answering questions

Business associations and clubs
If you belong to any business association or club, you might run across some new members who are looking for housing. If you're comfortable revealing that you own property it might be a good contact for you.

Neighborhood bulletin boards
Local neighborhood bulletin boards never seemed to catch the attention of good prospective renters for me, but that doesn't mean they should be overlooked. If that or other gathering spots seem to attract the kind of resident you're looking for - then advertise there.

Newspaper ads
I usually used newspaper ads as a last resort. They were very expensive and seldom worked well enough relative to the price I paid. If I did use them, it was only for the weekend: Friday, Saturday, and Sunday.

Your own residents
Some landlords have been successful by offering cash incentives to their residents if they bring in new renters. It never worked for me, but that does not mean you shouldn't try it yourself.

Chapter Summary:

Before you can begin the six-step process to select the right ~~tenant~~ resident, you must get them in the door. That begins with a number of advertising and marketing steps, as well as making sure your property has attractive amenities. Volume is the name of the game. The more preselected potential renters you have to choose from, the better your chances of success.

TENANT SELECTION: THE KEY INGREDIENT TO SUCCESS

David was the first realtor I worked with when I first got into the business. He usually worked in the Uptown district, which was an up and coming area just south of downtown Minneapolis in Minnesota. He understood people better than buildings. He gave me _the best advice I have ever received then - or since._

David's advice was simple yet brilliant:
" 90% of your problems will come from tenants. The rest will just be mechanical and can be easily fixed."

He went on to explain that bad residents can be a headache that never go away. If you have reliable repair people and contractors then the mechanical issues or repairs can be made quickly, paid for, and forgotten. A bad resident will not be forgotten until they have left your building. Sometimes not even then.

There is another equation here too - the emotional and psychological challenges of dealing with another human being. No matter what the problems or issues might be concerning this resident, they will usually never see it as 'their' problem. It will be either your 'fault' as the landlord/owner, circumstances beyond their control i.e. they could not pay the rent because they lost their job or had a big car repair bill due.

The only way I have found to reduce the potential problems with renters is to be extremely selective with them in the first place. It is time consuming, tiring, and can be very frustrating. Ultimately, it is the only way to eliminate (to a degree) this problem.

> **Introverts Like Me**
>
> I loathed this process of selecting residents because I'm an introvert and people skills have always been a major challenge to me. I realized very early in this game that resident selection was going to be essential to my success.

Resident selection is the toughest part of your job and the most critical to your long-term success.

I cannot emphasize enough that you MUST be discerning in your selection of residents.

Let me be clear about what I mean by 'discerning.' You cannot nor should you ever *discriminate* based on race, national origin, ancestry, religion, sex, familial status, or physical disabilities. Not only is it wrong and illegal, it is just simply bad business. You are trying to find the right mix of residents in your units. Those factors have no relevance in that resident selection…whatsoever.

Be sure to check your local anti-discrimination laws to be sure that some other factors have not been missed here, along with all the appropriate rental statutes in your area. You can stay on the right side of the law and still be very selective in determining who stays in your units.

Now, having said that you cannot discriminate on those factors, you owe it to yourself to be highly selective and in fact, *discriminate* against anyone whom you feel does not meet your criteria as a new resident or would not be a good fit for your building. Let me explain:

Everyone has issues. Some are more apparent or even shockingly obvious. Some are more subtle and cannot be recognized right away. It is your job, NO; it is your responsibility to examine each of your rental candidates in the most thorough manner possible. The last thing you want to do is make a bad resident selection and have to live with that mistake for a year or longer.

California and New York have some of the toughest tenant protection laws in the country. I owned properties in California and Minnesota. Minnesota, where the majority of my properties were located, also has stringent laws about what a property owner could and could not do to evict a renter. In almost every state in this country, the laws are always tilted IN FAVOR of the renter. It is simply much easier to find a good resident than it is to take a chance and have to live with your mistake and the consequences afterwards.

In the real world, there are people who are not able or willing to live with other folks. They carry with them baggage of every imaginable origin; mental, emotional, psychological, etc. There are also people who are anti-social or should never live in a communal environment. I had a phrase I used to describe those people who simply could not get along with others. "Trash is trash is trash and it all equals nothing but problems." It sounds harsh and perhaps on one level it is but remember here - we're talking about creating an atmosphere in your buildings where everyone has to live together and get along. You owe it to yourself to make sure you find the very best candidates to fill that requirement.

You are not just renting out units. You are providing safe, secure, and pleasant surroundings in which for them to live. You do not want to suddenly intrude on their surroundings and sense of security with bad neighbors.

Those sound like damning words, but in the real world we are talking about someone moving into one of your units for a minimum of one year or 365 days. Trust me; even one day of resident trouble is not worth the rent you are getting from any bad apples.

Don't be a social worker
Simply stated, there are folks who cannot afford your rent. They may be nice pleasant folks. They may be down on their luck. They may need a break. They may promise that a job is forthcoming. Future promises do not equate to a solid job that can pay the rent…today. It sounds cruel not to help your fellow man or woman. Nevertheless, your role is not that of social worker. You do not have those skills and your other residents deserve a new neighbor that is going to fit in and be like them - able to pay the rent.

Don't be a den mother
Some young folks had never been away from home before they came knocking on my door. While they were pleasant and sincere, they needed a mother hen or dorm mother to look over their first venture into independent living. That wasn't me.

I seldom rented to students. When they came calling, I always made it very clear that while it was never on a 'first come, first serve' basis in terms of filling out the rental application, I would certainly consider them if they had a good rental history elsewhere.

I made exceptions, but only after years of experience when my gut told me those folks were well educated, sincere, and quickly grasped the concept of their unit being a home and not a dorm room.

Beware of (some) pets
I learned very quickly that people who have cats would not give them up. I simply made sure they signed a separate pet application/policy and promised to keep their cat in their unit at all times. Usually that was sufficient for the both of us.

People who have dogs are a different breed. Most of them are very defensive about their animals and will say anything to convince you that their dog is quiet, will never bark, will not chew on anything, or crap in your front lawn. All of which are lies. Dogs are dogs. They do what they want to do.

Having said that, I did make the occasional exception. One of my best residents had dogs the entire time she lived in the building, almost twenty years. She walked them at least twice a day. She picked up after them and was super-conscious about their behavior relative to the other residents.

There are some breeds that you may not be able to accept due to insurance regulations alone. They include breeds like Pit Bulls, Rottweilers, German Shepherds, Alaskan Malamute, Doberman Pinscher, Chow, Great Dane, Saint Bernard, Akita and Wolf hybrids.

Be sure to check with your insurance carrier to see just what your own policy will and will not allow. Know that those dog owners will not understand that reasoning and will smell discrimination against Fido right from the start.

Dog owners NEVER think their animal will be a problem. Other dogs might cause issues but never theirs. It is not your job to argue with them. That is an argument you will never win. Just be firm that they were not chosen to live in your unit and NEVER say it had to do with their dog.

Use your head and not your heart
Over a period of thirty years, I would occasionally run into someone who wanted to rent from me that I could not accept. It was never a case of discriminating against someone because of race, gender, creed, or sexual orientation.

I made it very clear to anyone who walked into my lobby that this was not a dorm room, a party house, or a crash pad. Most of those coming to apply understood that right up front because of my phone conversation with them. Occasionally someone would come along who hadn't been quite upfront with me over the phone.

During the course of our conversation at the building or after they'd filled out the application form, it became apparent that they either didn't have a job, no rental history, past issues with other landlords, a problem dog, or something that brought up a red flag against their qualifications.

Some of them would argue that a job was soon forthcoming, that their dog really was not a problem, or that the other landlord was the 'real' problem. It was NEVER their problem, always someone else.

Sometimes single parents came along with several children. They always promised me that their kids were perfect, well behaved, and supervised. But with the only parent working full time, I doubted that was the case. If they had a good rental history, that could sway my decision in their favor. However, if they had no rental history or if it was sketchy, I always demurred and said no. I usually felt bad about turning them down but it was better to find someone better suited to the building than chancing future problems down the line. As long as I did not discriminate against them because of their children, I was legally entitled to choose whom I wanted to live in my buildings.

On the flip side of that turn-down, I probably had at least half a dozen single parents with children in my units. They always had a solid rental history and great references. I was never disappointed in any of them nor were there ever any problems.

The same was true for college students. I had, over the years, some terrific young people living in my buildings. They were quiet, courteous, and always respectful of others. Yet they had a ton of friends over, had parties, outdoor gatherings, and acted as young folks do today. They were never a problem.

The secret is that either they all came with a good rental history or their actions spoke highly of their maturity and understanding of communal living. Of course, some of them did not understand the concept of a pilot light in the stove or closing storm windows during the winter months. Overall, they were fun to have around and always willing to pitch in to help their older neighbors.

Stereotypical renters
Look for your own special brand of stereotypes that you like. My typical and best renters were young, educated, 'nice' people. You know who the nice people are. They are

pleasant, personable, open minded and understand that it is communal living we're talking about here. It is not a dorm, or 'animal house' or their crash pad back off campus. Most of my renters were the pre-cursers to today's millennials, yet they exhibited many of the same interests as young people do today.

My stereotypical renter liked riding bikes, the outdoors, urban gardening, conservation, sustainability, energy efficiency, engaging in all kinds of media entertainment, and socializing with their neighbors.

Do everything you can to attract and keep the stereotype that works for you and your building. When they take ownership in their unit, the building itself becomes part of their domain. They care about the cleanliness of the front lobby, the basement utility room, the front of the building and the back too.

When the Yard is not just a Yard

I can remember the first time I got a call from one of my residents who wanted to plant a garden behind her building. I have always been interested in gardening but seldom successful. Back at home, my mulch pile just stunk up the back yard and produced very little in the way of good fertilizer. I would forget to water the vegetables and the rabbits ate my flowers. I had accepted horticultural defeat a long time ago.

When this resident asked to dig up a small plot in back and plant some lettuce, tomatoes and other vegetables who was I to say no. Once the plot got started, other residents asked to join in her effort. It became a communal plot. My only caveat was that if it were not used, I would turn it back to grass.

It never went back to grass. Even if that first resident left, there always seemed to be another resident in another unit who wanted to start up the garden the next spring. They shared gardening tools and used my extra tools that I left downstairs in one spot in the laundry room.

Another resident wanted to plant flowers. I paid for the flowers and she bought them, planted them, trimmed them, and cleaned out the pots at the end of the season.

One time I went to the building and there was a volleyball net tied up in back. No problem as long as the other residents didn't object. They never did. I would also find groups of chairs and card tables where my residents had a building-wide picnic or card party outdoors during the summer months.

THE SIX-STEP PROCESS TO RENTING

There are very specific steps you must take to rent out a unit. This six-step process will allow you to spot and eliminate potential problem renter's right from the start. Much like perusing job applications, it is not an exact science, but instead one that was honed by me over the years. It puts the balance of power in your hands where it belongs and not in the hands of the prospective renter.

Step One: Attracting Quality Residents
The first step is to create a property that is competitively

attractive in the current rental market, then to advertise in a variety of ways that will attract the largest number of prospective quality candidates. I detailed these methods in the previous section.

You have to work the numbers in order to find good people. The more traffic you generate over the phone or that goes through your unit, the better your chances are that you will find the ideal prospects for that unit. It is time consuming and it can be frustrating but it must be done that way.

Step Two: Screening Phone Calls
The phone number I used was my business phone. During the time when my ad campaign was going on, I NEVER answered the phone. I always relied on the answering machine or voicemail to record all incoming calls.

By having prospective renters leave a message instead of talking directly with me I could determine a number of things.

I listened for background noises such as screaming kids, loud parties, etc. After a while, I could almost envision what those candidates were like in terms of their level of education, etc. The more information they left, the better I could ascertain whether I would return their calls. The reality is that most people fall into certain categories and I instinctively knew what I was looking for in a prospective resident.

Did I miss some good candidates by this screening process? I probably did. However, it also eliminated potential problems or candidates who did not fulfill my requirements right from the start. It was worth losing a few good prospects in the process.

Step Three: Make the Call-Back
When I called those prospects back that I had chosen from all the call-ins, I made a real effort to sound pleasant, sincere, and very friendly. There was a very serious purpose to that approach.

There are several examples of casual conversational questions meant to reveal deeper information from prospective residents. This very casual approach was meant to disarm most prospects. I wanted to make them feel comfortable and usually ready to tell me just about anything I needed to know about them. My call-back questions were purposely meant to sound casual and non-threatening and simply inquiring. This IS NOT AN INTERVIEW over the phone, just casual banter back and forth. So learn to ask each question in a relaxed manner - then shut up and LISTEN.

Question: *Are you renting right now?*
You're trying to find out:
Where they are renting.
How long they've been there.
If they've rented before.
If they live in a dorm or with their parents.
Their current living situation, such as living with roommates or a new boyfriend or girlfriend.

Question: *Where are you renting?*
You're trying to find out:
What part of town do they live in now; is it a good neighborhood, a bad neighborhood, expensive part of town, downtown or in the suburbs.
If they live in the suburbs do they anticipate a difference

between living in the city vs. the suburbs.
If they're from out of town, ask them to describe their current neighborhood or if they can compare to something in your town.

Question: *Why are you choosing to move now?*
You're trying to find out:
If there are any problems with a current landlord or other residents.
Issues with the building they're living in or that neighborhood.
This might also raise issues with their current living situation that might have to be addressed in your building (e.g. handicap needs, etc. student housing.)
You are also listening for anything that might have happened in their life that would warrant such a move. For example: loss of a job, romantic breakup, moving out of home, etc.

Question: *Where are you working now?*
You're trying to find out:
If it is a professional job, laborer, etc.
If it is part time or full time
If the prospective resident is liable to be laid off (seasonal work).
If the company is a stable operation or a government/union job with long-term job security.
A sense of how much the job pays (without asking, and before they fill out an application) so you can gauge if they can truly afford the rent you are asking for.

I wanted candidates to clearly understand what I was offering them. A quiet and peaceful place to call *home*, where neighbors are respectful of one another If they sounded agreeable and understanding of that mindset, then the conversation continued. If they did not, I made sure that I couldn't set up an appointment and promised to call them back ... which I never did.

On the surface, it sounds unfair and to a degree, it probably was. I am sure I missed some wonderful renters who went elsewhere. Nevertheless, the bottom line is that I was able to eliminate a number of prospective renters who would not have fit into my building... simple as that.

Step Four: Show the Unit
If I had been diligent in following the first three steps, I usually had a good feeling for any prospective renter who walked up my front sidewalk. Of course, there was always the exception when a sweet-sounding thing walked up toward my front door accompanied by her skinhead boyfriend or gang of party girls.

My first three steps *usually* worked - but not always.

The tour of the unit is the next critical step. By now, candidates have been pre-screened. They sound like they would be right for the unit and therefore the building. Now the proof is in the pudding. Will they like the unit? Will they like you? Do you like them once you meet them in person?

I would greet them as they walked up the front steps. I shook their hands (and those of anyone else who might be accompanying them). We stood in the lobby for a moment as I introduced the building, number of units, and a few other sundry notes of interest. Then we walked into the available unit.

It was imperative that the current renters be out of their unit when I showed it. Ninety-nine percent of the time, the current renters were very amenable to being gone when their unit was being shown.

As we walked through the front door of the unit, I always stepped aside and let the prospects take the lead. I was there to answer their questions but not lead them on. Of course, as they toured the unit, I was very observant about everything they said and did. Again, most prospects would fall into the same categories.

The 'lookers' would walk through the unit very quickly and determine almost immediately if they were interested or not. If not, they would ask to see the rest of the building but we both understood from that point on that it was just a waste of their time and mine.

The 'serious candidates' took their time in examining each room. They asked many questions and made a point to let me know they were interested in renting the unit.

Questions were the first and most important way of determining a candidate's level of interest. The more questions asked, the more serious they were. The fewer questions, the more likely they weren't interested or they had more units on their list to see first.

By the time it came for me to offer them an application form, I could usually tell if they were interested or not. Nevertheless, EVERYONE got the offer of an application form whether they asked for it or not.

There were several points I emphasized to them about the application form itself.
A. There was no fee involved for them.
B. I would follow through on verifying all information.
C. Blank spaces were suspect and false info meant the form

was thrown out immediately.
D. It is not first-come, first-served. I was looking for the right resident to fit within the community of this particular building.

ANYONE who wanted to live in one of my units had to fill out an application form. I had the occasional excuse that their prospective roommate was abroad or unavailable. In that case, I patiently explained to them that IF their prospective roommate did not fill out the form and did not pass my investigation, they wouldn't be allowed in the unit. That usually dissuaded those folks from continuing the application process.

Remember that there are always more reasons to reject someone than there are to approve them. I have rented to all genders, married and unmarried, straight and gay, kids and no kids, pets and no pets, cops and lawyers. Every one of them had to fill out an application form and pass mustard. No exceptions!

Step Five: Examining the Application Form
Your most basic application form should include:

- Name(s)
- Age
- Sex
- Current employer (with complete address)
- Work supervisor's name and number
- Job title, salary, and employed since date
- Number of months or years on the job
- A second past employer (optional)
- Present address
- Home phone
- Current rent

- Utilities included in current rent or not
- Landlord name / phone
- Their reasons for moving out of their current place.
- Automobile information.
- Credit information (as legally available).
- Banking information (as legally available).
- Emergency numbers.

The last line should read: "If accepted, I understand that this application shall be attached to my rental agreement, and further state that the above information is true and correct to the best of my knowledge."

I ALWAYS followed through in verifying every line on that form.

When calling a past landlord, ask about the prospect's current rental history, any past problems, and most importantly:

Are they respectful?
and
Would you rent to them <u>again</u>?

In today's litigious society, most landlords understand that they have to be very careful about what they say about past or current renters. If I am talking to another landlord and he or she seems hesitant to say anything about their current renter, I always ask, "Would you rent to this person again?" That is ALL I asked. I don't ask for their reasoning or past issues or current problems. IF they say they would rent to them again, I answer: 'thank you' and let it go at that. If they say no, I answer 'thank you' and let it go at that. They've told me ALL I need to know.

If some lines on the application form seem questionable and I am still interested in that candidate, I will call them back and ask for an explanation or more information. The honest ones will quickly comply. Those who are trying to hide something will not.

The rental application itself
No one rental application is the best. There are literally dozens and dozens of forms that can be copied from many different sources. You need to decide which best suits your needs and will give you a very clear picture of the kind of person who intends to rent from you. I recommend:
1. Go back to the landlord before the current one.
2. Clear job references and a boss or two to call…salary and other income listed.
3. Have a separate application for pets if you are going to accept them.
4. Have a separate application if the prospective resident is also renting a garage or extra space in your building.
5. Clearly state which expenses are the responsibility of the owner and which are for the renter.
6. Clearly state penalties for late payments or bad checks.
7. Clearly state what changes can or can't be made in the unit including painting, carpeting, remodeling, etc.

Step Six: Sign the Lease and Collect the Money
By now, you've gone through all the steps to find the very best candidate for your unit.

At this point, you need to finalize things by having them sign the lease agreement, collect their security deposit, and answer any lingering questions they may have about the unit, the building, or neighborhood.

I always met my candidates back at the building because

more often than not, they would want to see the building again, walk through their unit, perhaps to measure rooms, see the basement and outside grounds again. I always tried to introduce them to my other residents if they were available. We would discuss their move-in time frame and all the necessary details of living in the building.

I encouraged them to call me with their questions and made it a point of being around when they actually moved in. It was very important that they understood right up front that I was an active and very involved property owner and I meant every word I said about myself, the other residents, and the building itself.

It's not done until it's done
The last step of actually signing the lease agreement and handing over the security deposit is usually the easiest. Those residents have been screened. They're excited about moving into their unit and you're excited about having them as residents.

I've only had a couple of occasions where that procedure didn't quite go as planned. One fellow showed up, signed the lease agreement, and then said he first wanted to have it checked out by a lawyer. That was the first time he'd mentioned a lawyer in our many conversations. My gut told me he just wanted out. Therefore, I gave him twenty-four hours or I would declare that agreement null and void since I hadn't signed it yet. He disappeared just as my gut told me he would.

Another time a woman showed up to sign the lease but then announced that she would be paying her rent on a weekly basis instead of a monthly basis. I told her that if she couldn't or wouldn't pay on a monthly basis, my offer of the unit would be rescinded. She also promptly disappeared and never called me again.

A couple of times a young couple or single woman would show up with their parents in tow. Usually the parents understood their role as that of an observer but occasionally they didn't. If I felt they (usually the father) were stepping beyond their roles in the transaction, I would tell them so. However, usually it was the resident who would shut them up first...for fear of losing the unit.

These were exceptions to the rule. If I had done my job well in screening the applicants, then this last step was a breeze. If I hadn't and there were problems I always felt it was better to face the issue head-on before they moved into the unit rather than after they were established there.

Lease vs. rental agreement
A typical rental agreement commits your resident to a short rental period, typically on a month-to- month basis. There is no long term commitment on either one of your parts and frees you up to cancel the agreement at any time within the appropriate time frame. It also means your resident can also leave at any time. Anytime includes the middle of winter when it can be very difficult to re-rent the unit.

In my mind, the positive aspects of a rental agreement don't make up for the potential problems it might also entail. I would only go with a lease on a yearly basis and nothing less.

Security deposits
Most often, the security deposit is the same amount as the monthly rent. It is due, in full, upon signing of the lease agreement. Under no circumstances should you ever accept any amount less than the full amount due for the security deposit. If they can't pay it, they shouldn't be allowed to rent your unit.

The same is true for monthly payments. I never accepted bi-weekly payments. It was always due at the end of the month. Once you begin accepting bi-weekly checks, it is far too easy for residents to become lax about when the rent is due and it makes your recordkeeping a total nightmare.

Both state law and often city ordinances regulate security deposits. They usually earn some kind of interest while they're being held by the landlord. They may have to be held in a separate account from others and usually cannot be used to pay the last month's rent. Laws vary with each state and you must know and abide by those rules for security deposits.

Once the resident moves out, you usually have from 14 to 30 days to return the deposit along with interest earned. If deductions are made from that amount, an itemized list must be provided with expenses against that amount and the final amount paid back to the resident.

Scams and lies
Usually anyone looking to rent from me had been through the rental process before. They understood the need for a security deposit and while the actual amount might vary from one landlord to another, the overall process remained the same.

Occasionally, someone would come along who claimed to love the building, claimed to have great credentials, and really wanted to live there. It all sounded great until they casually mentioned that they always paid their security deposit in increments instead of upfront at one time. They made it sound like an everyday occurrence. When I said no it had to be paid in its entirety up front, they always disappeared.

Others claimed to be just starting a new job but wouldn't

give me the name and number of their new employer. A few were starting their own business but wouldn't show my any financials. A couple of young men said they were renting space from their parents in the basement of their home. They assured me their parents would highly recommend them as residents.

Oftentimes, the scams varied but always fell into the same pattern. These potential renters could not or would not follow the rules that I had set forth. They urged me to make them an exception and always, always promised to pay on time. In every instance, I smiled and said no. No exceptions were my rule and I stuck to it.

RESIDENT MAINTENANCE

Late fees
My lease agreement always had a late fee penalty for late rent checks and yet I don't believe I ever pressed the issue. My residents were great people and if a check was late, I usually accepted their explanation for why that happened. It made for good resident relations not to push the issue. Of course, if there were any penalties from the bank due to a bounced check, that cost was passed on to the resident. In the end, I always got paid and the residents had no reason to get mad at me.

Vacancies
I probably had a total of six months of vacancies over a 30-year period. I tried to avoid them at almost all costs. The reason is simple; you can never make up one month's loss of rent – period.

That's why the selection process is so very important. Not only do you avoid (generally speaking) issues with problem residents, you keep your cash flow steady and reliable.

Managing rents

Be reasonable about raising your rents.

Some landlords I knew raised their rents every year no matter how good or how long the resident had been in a unit. Their philosophy was simple: "They (the residents) expect it and I need the money." More often than not, what happened was a vacancy at the end of that lease and the principled landlord had to begin the leasing process all over again.

In my mind, it was a very simple equation. One month's loss of rent couldn't be made up no matter how high I raised the rents in the future. Mind you, I always raised the rent on a unit that was going to be vacated so that it was current with other rents nearby.

If a resident wanted to stay for another year, I certainly was not about to dissuade them from staying by raising their rent. Instead, I emphasized to them that if they stayed for another year, I would not raise their rent…period.

If a resident had been in their unit for several years, then a rent increase was not unreasonable or unexpected. The key here is to be reasonable.

I seldom raised rents more than five to ten dollars per month. More than that and residents won't understand it. They only see it from their perspective, never from yours.

By following this policy and studying local comps, I made sure that my rents were always average or below average. Having said that, I would compare my vacancy rate with anyone else and always come out ahead.

Two Good Examples

There were two residents, both on opposite ends of the livability and personality spectrum who were a good example of why to be cautious about raising rents.

The first was a young man who lived in one of my basement units for over sixteen years. He went through an average of a job a year and yet always paid his rent on time.

There were several occasions when one of his rent checks would bounce, but he always made good on it along with the bank's penalty charge.

Over the years, I hired him to shovel for me, cut the grass, do some odd jobs and overall just watch out for the building. Yet to the untrained eye, this fellow was on the surface a very questionable resident.

He kept very strange hours and one never knew if he was sleeping during the day, had disappeared for short periods of time or simply never followed the routine patterns of my other residents. To say that he led a very strange lifestyle would be an understatement.

His apartment unit was a total disaster.

He collected cans and papers and he had large black garbage bags strewn throughout his unit. He slept on his couch and never cleaned or dusted his unit. He blocked off one room and used it to store all kinds of strange items. Dishes piled up and spilled out of his kitchen sink. To walk through his unit was like walking through a disaster movie.

Since very few potential renters wanted to live in a basement unit (women especially), I was reticent to let him go just because I didn't understand or approve of the way he lived. I seldom raised his rent and he stayed around for sixteen years. That was sixteen years I didn't have to worry about a vacant basement apartment and sixteen years I could rely on him to watch out for the building.

Yet for all of his outward appearances of disunity, this fellow's unit NEVER had a problem with bugs, roaches, ants, mice, etc. If a check was late, he made it up promptly. If a check bounced, he made it up promptly. As long as I overlooked his strange and sometimes unconventional lifestyle, he was a great resident.

One time I left for three weeks to tour Asia and I gave him the keys to all my buildings. There were a couple of occasions when a problem arose in my absence. He called the plumbers or electricians, got the work done, paid the bills for me and covered my tush while I was gone. You couldn't ask for better service than that.

The other good example was a middle-aged woman who came with her dog. While I was usually very hesitant to rent to someone with a dog, she made it very clear that she wasn't about to leave her dog behind. She had a good rental history and I talked to her old landlord specifically about her dog. He assured me that the dog hadn't been a problem.

I took a chance on her. She became, without a doubt, one of my best residents ever. She stayed in my building for over twenty years and I loved having her there. She watched the building like a hawk.

If a light bulb burnt out or there were issues with other residents she was the first to let me know. She became my eyes and ears and took ownership of the building right from the start.

Shortly after she moved in, she got married to a lawyer. Now most landlords would be leery about having an attorney in one of their units. Her new husband was as charming, kind, considerate, and responsible as she was. Together they made a wonderful couple and great residents in my building.

I very seldom raised her rent. She was too good a resident to chase away just because I wanted to make an extra buck.

There were some others like her and that fellow who turned out to be such good residents that I seldom raised their rent and if I did, it was never more than $5.00 or $10.00 a month.

WHAT IF THIS RESIDENT DOESN'T WORK OUT?

What to do when residents must leave unexpectedly
If you've done your job well and were diligent in your resident selection then the problem of how to get rid of folks usually doesn't crop up very often. If it does occur in the middle of a lease, there are very specific steps to take.

More often than not, there is usually some crisis in their lives that is causing the issue at hand. It might be a crisis of their making or something outside of their control. Either way, it has to be addressed.

This is where you need to be flexible in terms of the lease agreement and your willingness to break the lease to end the problem at hand. The circumstances may vary but generally fall into two categories.

Justified Reasons to Break a Lease
First, the resident has a legitimate reason to move out of the unit. They've gotten a new job. They are getting divorced or separating from their partner. No matter the reason, their life has changed and requiring them to pay off the rest of their lease will only cause issues for both you and them. I was always firm in their paying for their lease until a new one was signed and I was guaranteed no break in the flow of cash from that unit.

On the other hand, I wasn't about to insist that they pay off the rest of the lease. In reality, they probably would have moved out to another state and I'd never get paid anything. Try collecting past due rent from someone who has moved out of state…hard to impossible. Besides, if you appear fair with them, 99% of them will respond in kind.

Understandable Reasons to Break a Lease
Roommate issues, loss of a job or personal issues are all reasons outside of the lease agreement that might affect their ability or willingness to stay in the unit. In almost every instance, the present resident NEVER saw it as their problem or responsibility. It was always the fault of the other person. No matter the reason, if they are dead set on moving, then you have to be just as firm in stating the terms under which they can leave.

Non-Legitimate Reasons to Break a Lease
There is a third category such as buying a home or finding a better unit that are not legitimate reasons to break the lease.

A few residents simply aren't smart enough to understand that. I've had arguments with a few residents who thought they could break their lease because they meet someone new and wanted to move in with them. Perhaps Mom and Dad had just given them the down payment for a house and they wanted out of their lease.

In any of these instances, the fact that the resident is moving must be addressed nevertheless. Again, I was firm about not losing any rent during this transitional period. By not insisting they pay out the rest of their lease, we avoided World War III and we both got what we wanted. They got to move out without having to pay off the rest of their lease and I didn't lose any money in the process.

In a few instances, you can sense that issues are brewing but can't pinpoint exactly what they are. In almost every case, the pattern becomes the same. The resident doesn't return your inquiring phone call. They will lie to you about probable causes or issues.

All you can do in those instances is be persistent and make sure you are paid your rent on time.

How to Get Rid of Residents
Fortunately, I only had a few instances where I was determined to get rid of a resident.

The causes may have varied but ultimately it was no longer a good fit and we would both be better off if they were gone. Of course, in most instances, they didn't see themselves as the problem and they usually wanted to stay. Remember the bad ones NEVER see themselves as the problem. It is always circumstances beyond their control, outside influences, temporary issues, etc.

I would always follow a very clear pattern and never deviate from it. First, I would give them a three-month notice in writing and in person. I would talk to them and present them with the letter that simply stated that I wasn't going to renew their lease and they would have to vacate their unit by the end of their present lease.

Most of them would insist that I tell them the reason for my actions. I NEVER DID. In Minnesota, a landlord does not have to give a reason for not renewing a lease. I never wanted to give them any ammunition to use against me in the future. It would not have mattered WHAT reason I gave for my actions, they would have argued against it. Remember (and I know I'm being redundant here) in their mind, it is never their fault.

I simply said to them, "I have chosen not to renew your lease." The fact of the matter is that 99% knew exactly why I wasn't renewing their lease but wouldn't admit it even if strapped to a lie detector machine. That was probably one of their problems; embracing denial in their life.

A couple of them got very mad and made it difficult for me to show their unit. In those few instances, I would either offer the unit to someone else in the building or be willing to lose a month's rent in order to avoid any confrontation between current resident and prospective renter.

The lesson to remember here is that every resident that left one of my units (I can count less than four with whom I had this issue) did so with the feeling that they had gotten the best of me. They got out of their lease or unit and could move on. I wanted them to feel that way. There was no way that I wanted them to feel they had been screwed by me. The chance of them returning to do damage to my building was something that scared me to death.

Yet in every instance of their leaving, I'm convinced they

went to another apartment building and surprise, surprise, they encountered another landlord who was also a jerk.

Since any issues that arose were never their fault, it simply made sense that the next landlord was their newest problem. Most importantly, they were no longer MY problem...end of story. I rented out their unit to someone nicer, at a higher rent and life moved on...that is mine did. I expect their lives continued to be filled with issues, problems, and other jerks.

She Shall Remain Anonymous

There have only been a couple of really bad residents whom I had to get rid of. In those rare instances, the pattern usually remained the same. They started out great. I thought they would fit in well with the other residents. They expressed strong interest in being there. Then something went south.

One woman in particular was a real problem. She had developed a pattern of late rent checks or checks that bounced on a regular basis. Of course, it was never her fault but instead that of the postal service, the bank, her employers or the alignment of the sun. BUT never was it her fault.

She argued with me that I could NOT not rent to her and then demanded written proof of her sins as a cause for me not to renew. I quietly and gently pointed out to her that there were no laws on the books in Minnesota that said I HAD to have a reason for not renewing her lease.

She overstayed the end of her lease by five days but fortunately, I hadn't rented her unit for the next month. When she moved out five days late, she stiffed me with her electric bill. Yet because of her erratic and sometimes scary behavior, I let it all go.

She finally left believing that I was the devil incarnate. I was joyful to have her out of my building. Her unit was rented out for a lot more than she had been paying and that increase covered all of the expenses she left me with. I'm guessing she went on to another apartment building and found that landlord to be just as much a jerk as she felt I was. I got a new wonderful renter in her place, at a higher rent and peace back in the building.

Guess who won in the end?

Do Onto Others
The one truth I learned from over thirty plus years of owning and managing apartment buildings is that the more I could do for my residents, the more they felt inclined to do for themselves. Simply stated, you do right by doing good. Once my renters knew I cared, they cared…it is as simple as that.

> **Merry Christmas and Happy Hanukkah**
>
> Every Christmas/Hanukkah I would leave a gift box for every unit (cookies, candy, etc.). I didn't do it because I had to. I did it because I wanted to. I saw all my renters as great residents. I appreciated them being in my buildings and I wanted them to stay.

You don't have to give gifts at Christmas time to attract or keep good residents. But if you treat them with respect...*all the time* ... they will know and appreciate it. If that becomes part of your operating philosophy, you are well on your way to success in managing apartment buildings.

Chapter Summary:
The most crucial element in managing small apartment buildings is **resident selection** and **resident maintenance**. Nothing else comes close in terms of problem avoidance and a continuation of cash flow. There are specific steps to take in resident selection; each is important and together they will help you find the best fit for each building.

FINANCIALS AND RECORDKEEPING

My Financial Route to Purchasing Buildings

My personal journey into investments took a circuitous route around and through some very bad investment vehicles before I discovered what worked best for my personality.

Looking back, I am embarrassed with some of the investments my wife and I initially made around that time. We were talked into some penny stocks without having any idea what penny stocks were or knowing what our chances were of seeing any kind of investment return. We bought diamonds, again on the advice of friends, and only got out of that one just in time. We were encouraged to buy into antiquities and other exotic investments. We were constantly barraged by stockbrokers offering to sell us everything from Australian currency to the latest fast food franchise.

Since I had always had an interest in real estate, I began to focus my attention in just that area. I decided I had to be a hands-on manager of my own investments because I simply did not trust someone else with them. That attitude has mellowed over the years and now our portfolio is professionally managed and the ROI is commensurate with the rest of the industry.

At the time I began thinking of investing in small apartment buildings, I was working fulltime and had a small business on the side. I was also a young father with two small children, was involved in our community, and wanted to spend as much time with my kids as I could. It certainly helped that my wife was a stay-at-home mom during that period.

This was the pre-personal computer and internet era. There was very little written about this particular kind of real estate. In fact, most of what had been written up to that point was either focused on managing large apartment complexes or just generic information on real estate investments in general.

I began to talk to the few other folks I knew who owned small apartment buildings. There was a fledgling organization in town that was comprised of just apartment owners. I attended some of their meetings and asked many questions. I began to talk to real estate agents who specialized in that area of real estate as compared to residential property sales.

Gradually I began to get a much better picture of the whole world of small apartment building management. I decided this was an area of investment I could control. It was in an area of real estate that I found fascinating, and I thought I might be able to manage it through focused time management.

I was right and I was wrong.

I made a ton of mistakes along the way - hence the reason for this guide.

I also learned from my mistakes and gradually I worked the management of my buildings into my lifestyle so I could still work full-time, manage my small business, find time for the kids, and still have a fulfilling life. I think if you follow these principles, you can do the same thing in your life.

Contract for Deed

My funding route was different from others who went straight to the bank for a loan. My business was generating a solid return, so I approached the owner of the first building with a proposal to buy his property through a CD; a Contract for Deed.

A Contract for Deed is an investment vehicle in which the original owner still owns the property until the mortgage is paid off over a period of time. The seller receives a monthly payment, principle, and interest, for a specified period. This is usually twenty years or so. In the meantime, the new buyer pays off the old owner and still enjoys all the benefits of owning the property outright.

In my case, I took money out of my business to make two twenty thousand dollar down payments over two years on the building. After that initial investment, the income generated by the building itself paid ALL future expenses and did so until the building was sold. Because this investment route worked out so well for me, I continued to follow that pattern with all future purchases of my apartment buildings.

Obtaining loans from other sources will change the equation here. The idea is to find a loan or down payment that will allow you to initially (or within a relatively short period of time) generate a positive cash flow for your building(s).

The idea that you can purchase a building with no money down and still generate a positive return and cash back into your pocket is generally speaking a rarity or an outright sham. While there may be an exception here and there, overall it is seldom done.

Buying property through a real estate agent

It is usually better to buy an apartment building through an agent who knows the history of the building, the seller, the neighborhood, and other factors that might prove critical when you become the new owner.

Partnership arrangements with multiple buyers
I've seldom heard of any partnership arrangement that didn't have its own set of unique issues and challenges for all the parties involved. For a first time buyer, it's usually wiser to buy that first property by yourself. You'll have a much steeper learning curve but it will be yours alone and not shared with anyone else.

Leverage
Unlike most other investments, leverage is the key to real estate investing. A little bit of cash can buy you a lot of real estate. In most cases, a down payment of ten to 20 percent is enough to get you into the business.

Leverage is the key to financing your purchase in today's financial environment, along with timing and location.

The down side is that you are highly leveraged and thus deeply in debt. The other side of that is the upside potential for a very nice return should your property increase in value. It can show high returns based on a relatively small up-front investment.

Whether your purchase is a Contract for Deed, a bank loan, or a group of investors as a limited liability company, you need to weigh all the benefits versus the risks before committing to one single approach.

Remember that realtors are camp followers. They will tell you anything to make the sale – trust no one – trust nothing they tell you – it's all up to you and your due diligence.

Homesteading

If your circumstances allow, then homesteading is another approach to consider.

Many investors don't know that small apartment buildings are perfect vehicles for homesteading. Homesteading is defined as property that is designated by a householder as the householder's home and protected by law from forced sale to meet debts.

Time value of money

For most real estate transactions, the majority of the purchase will be financed through various lending sources and/or institutions. Ultimately, the true cost of your purchase is not the sale price but the total amount you are required to pay over the length of the loan. Your true cost to purchase has more to do with the interest rate you pay than the price on the property.

Understanding interest rates, compounding interest and the positive effects of prepayments on a mortgage can go a long way toward selecting the best possible terms for your real estate purchase.

Once the price of the property has been established, then it is a question of pen to paper or calculator to computer to run the numbers and determine the best financial approach to take that meets your ultimate real estate goals.

Lending conditions change all the time and can vary from state to state or region to region. In this very fluid environment, it is important to be up-to-date on changing conditions and opportunities.

Negotiating

Before you can negotiate with either the seller or the agent, you must first know yourself better than anyone else. Each one of us has a unique personality and interacts differently with other people. You have strengths and weaknesses relative to your ability to out-think, out-talk, and out-negotiate other people. You must first know what your personal strengths and weaknesses are before exposing yourself to the negotiating game.

First and foremost, listen carefully and keep your mouth shut. There have been many deals that were squashed by potential buyers who couldn't keep their mouths shut. Listen carefully to the agent and anyone else present who has information that would be of benefit to you. Then be sure to ask a lot of questions.

One of the more popular opposing tactics is the 'straw man theory.' That is, if you don't jump at the deal, there are others waiting in the wings to grab it from you or there is a better price already on the table. Don't believe it!

If either of those statements were true, then the agent or seller wouldn't be bothering to talk to you. They would have grabbed the other deal or at least initiated a bidding war right from the start. If you are given this argument, simply smile and say nothing.

Trust your instincts, but make sure they are backed by solid facts. Don't assume your opponents have come to the same conclusions as you have. Find out what they know and how much they know about the deal during the process of the negotiations. But don't acknowledge this.

Never accept the first offer made. Always respond with a smile and nod, but always ensure that you study and analyze anything placed in front of you. Keep the pressure of time on them, not yourself.

If the offer is fair then see if you can get more concessions or add-ons to the deal. If so, good. If not, it never hurts to ask. You've negotiated the best deal for you and the seller or buyer has gotten what they asked for.

MARKERS OF A SUCCESSFUL BUSINESS

Every business enterprise is fraught with issues and opportunities. I have always subscribed to the belief that one of the keys to real financial and personal success in this business is how you manage your apartments for a maximum return on your investment while having a life worth living at the same time. It goes far beyond simply trusting your gut and flying by the seat of your pants. You need to manage your properties in such a manner that your residents pay for everything after your initial down payment has been made.

That means you have done a good job at resident selection. You do some of the necessary maintenance work yourself. You carefully manage your expenses. Lastly, you offer a better place to live so your residents stay and you don't have to deal with turnover and new resident selection. It's a lot of work upfront for an easier time afterwards. Remember, if your residents believe that you care about their home and their needs, they will respond in kind.

Recordkeeping
I used to laugh at my mother who always taped a little note on her new appliances and mechanicals in the basement. She wanted to remember when she had purchased that piece of equipment. In my foolish youth, I thought it was an odd and eccentric thing to do.

Little did I understand the wisdom of her ways until I got

into the business and suddenly had to be responsible for dozens of stoves, refrigerators, furnaces, water heaters, etc. On more than one occasion I found myself pondering the age of an appliance, where I had purchased it, whether I had an owner's manual stashed away somewhere and other basic questions of ownership. I was flying blind because I had no past records to examine.

It took me a long time to understand the wisdom and beauty of clear record keeping on each one of my units. With excel spreadsheets nowadays, it is easy to track all activities associated with a unit. This is true for the building as a whole from major mechanicals to landscaping and repairs, etc.

It is absolutely essential to track appliances and equipment over a period of time. The first time I had a question about the age of my own heating system, I suddenly realized that I had no idea because I hadn't kept adequate notes on the piece of equipment. My mother's exercise was time-tested, old fashioned and made sense because IT WORKED.

Right from the start, you must note every repair and replacement so that in the future you can determine the age of your appliances, past repairs, etc. Trust me, a month from now you will NOT remember what appliance you just replaced or repaired.

Once I had this record keeping system established, I could quickly and easily see when a particular unit had an appliance such as a stove or refrigerator installed, its repair history, its maintenance record, and anticipated life expectancy.

I could also track everything done to that particular apartment unit from painting, repairs, remodeling, any add-ons, and major or minor issues particular to it. In addition, I could review past comments made by residents and any comments they might have made about the unit that, in fact, became an issue with newer residents. This clearly defined history of each unit proved invaluable whenever an issue arose in the future. I'm sorry it took me so long to wise up and follow my mother's very wise behavior.

There is another aspect of record keeping that is critical to managing your properties. You must keep all your resident records – forever. You never know when a past resident might come calling for information about her tenancy in one of your units. I have records of EVERY resident plus my own personal notes on them, incidents, issues, etc. IF any one of them were ever to come back and challenge their rental history, I can prove my points in writing.

Legal Assistance
You don't need a lawyer on retainer unless you have hundreds of units, you're too stupid to handle simple issues yourself, or have no common sense. If an issue arises that might need legal help, you can always hire an attorney on an hourly basis to handle some particular problem.

My Biggest Failure

As I mentioned at the beginning of this section, I used to laugh at my Mother's odd habit of labeling all of her appliances and the mechanicals in her basement. While I understood her motivation and desire to keep a record of her purchases I saw little use for such an odd practice. That is not until I was well into my apartment management career. By then it was too late to rectify such an uninformed mistake.

If I was smart the first thing I should have done with the purchase of my first building was to literately label everything mechanical and to begin keeping detailed records of each appliance in every unit. That would include every stove, refrigerator, toilet, furnace, water heater, etc.

Insurance

If you own rental property, you could be sued for any reason - logical or illogical. That is a basic unpleasant fact in this business. Umbrella coverage is probably necessary in today's day and age. People sue even if they don't live in your building. Learn to keep detailed records and make every effort to show a caring response if something happens to one of your residents. Think ahead. For example; in cold climates during winter, have sand available for ice coverage and shovels to clear sidewalks before you can get there, etc.

Do everything you can to avoid or prevent an accident. Nevertheless, make sure you are covered by insurance.

There are only two things that might save your bacon from being sued. First, following the philosophy of this book, is to treat your residents well so that they are not inclined to sue you. Secondly, make sure you have umbrella coverage so that if issues arise, you have the proper financial reserves to cover any damages that might be awarded your residents or their guests in case of a dispute.

Taxes

Use taxes to your advantage. The objective here is tax avoidance, not evasion. Your goal is to maximize expenses and to minimize income within the boundaries of the law, both state and federal.

That takes excellent record keeping, personal notes, knowledge of local, city, county, state and federal tax laws and a very good accountant. IF I was going to be audited in the future, I wanted to be sure that I had impeccable records that went back at least 10 or more years.

Understand every legitimate deduction that you can take in managing and maintaining your building. It is well worth your time and effort to consult with other property owners and tax accountants to see just what you can do to get the maximum return on your investment in the building.

Chapter Summary:
Proper financial management and detailed record keeping are critical elements that affect both the bottom line and your return on investment (ROI). Computer technologies make today's recordkeeping easier and more accurate than ever before.

PROPERTY MAINTENANCE

In this section, you will learn how to put into place management strategies and key steps to enhance your resident's living experience and eliminating small mistakes that can lead to bigger problems. This, in turn, will give you a competitive edge on other competing apartment buildings and attract the kind of resident you are looking for.

When maintaining properties, you must build a cadre of reliable service providers and repair technicians to take care of your maintenance issues. If you manage your budget correctly, then the residents will end up paying all your bills.

Joining Together
In Saint Paul, Minnesota where many of my buildings were located, most city blocks have alleys separating the homes in back. It snows in Minnesota and sometimes it snows a lot. Residents expect to be able to get out of their buildings and if they own cars, they expect to be able to drive their cars to work or just to get out of the area.

Winter Wonderland

It was always my policy to have my sidewalks shoveled within hours after a major snowfall. Whether I did it myself or hired one of my residents, it was a policy that was strictly followed.

Hiring a snowplow operator individually can be a very expensive proposition. In my case, my other neighborhood owners and I were able to join together and hire a firm to plow our alley. It worked out well and saved all of us a lot of money. A few homeowners along the alley never bothered to join in, but that didn't mean it wasn't still the best option.

I also had occasion to purchase appliances together with other building owners. Group purchases usually worked out very well since we still got a warranty with the product, enjoyed a discount on a group purchase, and usually same-day installation since our respective buildings weren't that far apart. I also shared snow shoveling or lawn services when the opportunity arose. Any group purchase or sharing of services worked out well for all involved.

Do-it-yourself repairs vs. hiring the pros

I was never a handyman myself. Far from it. However, there were numerous tasks and chores around my buildings that I could teach myself to do instead of paying some service person to handle. If you can handle the maintenance, then by all means, do it yourself and save a lot of money. If you don't have the time or talent to make repairs, always go to your list of past proven repairmen and stick with them.

My philosophy with trades-people was exactly as it was with my residents. I treat all of them with total respect. I paid them on time and thanked them for their effort. In turn, they came to know my buildings and me. They trusted me and knew they would be paid promptly. It was a mutually beneficial relationship for both of us.

When I needed a repair done or service completed, I always insisted on being their 'first call' of the day. If not, it might have meant waiting hours for them to arrive.

Be a good customer
Use the same regular service professionals. Not only was treating them with respect the right thing to do it also meant that I was a regular customer to them. They could count on me for regular work and prompt payment. That in turn meant I could expect good service and fair scheduling.

Around the time I was winding down my business I noticed a disturbing trend among service providers. A lot of the 'old timers' that I had worked with for years were retiring and their children or associates were taking over the business. Unfortunately, some of the replacements didn't share the same passion and commitment to their work as the previous owners had. In those instances, I simply found other providers, but took the time to research them thoroughly.

In some instances, it was a third generation company where grandpa started the business and gained a good reputation. Then dad takes over and continues that tradition. Then when the third generation takes over, they think the business will run itself and they don't care about their customers. When that happens, it is time to bail.

Residents for hire
About the only thing I allowed my residents to do in their

respective units was painting. I paid for paint supplies and assumed that since it was their own unit, they would do a good job. I was almost always right. They were free to paint whatever they wanted as long as I approved of the color - which had to be something safe and not outlandish.

I seldom allowed or would pay for a resident to do maintenance or upkeep on their unit or the building itself. In those rare instances when I did allow a resident to do some work, they were only paid by a check from me. This was completely separate from their rent check.

Never deduct services from rent
I NEVER allowed them to deduct a part of their rent for their work.

One of my cardinal rules that I never wavered from was that if a resident did any work in their unit or the building in general, I would pay them with a separate check. It never came out of their rent due at the end of the month.

If someone wanted to cut the grass for me or shovel the snow I would only agree to it if they had been a long term resident and proven their reliability. Again, I paid them promptly with a **separate** check.

The Paint Store

I learned a big lesson before I formulated my response to this request.

It happened when one of my first renters wanted to paint her bedroom. She was a very pleasant and responsible woman so I thought *what could possibly go wrong?* I told her to go ahead, buy the supplies and I would reimburse her for her expenses.

A month later, she presented me with a bill of $285.00 for paint supplies for one small bedroom. That was back in the early 80's. Even today that would be a considerable bill. I was flabbergasted until I realized that she had been taken to the cleaners.

Upon my agreement to let her paint her small bedroom, the woman marched down to her local paint shop and told them: "My landlord is paying for painting supplies for my bedroom, what do I need to do the job?

Her bill included several drop clothes (the room was only 10 by 12), numerous paint pads, rags, buckets, primer, the most expensive paint they had, more paint than she could ever use on such a small area and an assortment of other items for her painting pleasure. Since she had never painted anything before she had no idea that she (really me!) was being taken for a ride.

I paid her bill because I had promised to do so but never again would I allow anyone to order supplies for me. In the future if someone wanted to paint their room or apartment, I always insisted (really demanded) that I buy all the paint supplies ahead of time.

Replacing appliances and other items for your properties
Appliances, the furnace system, the hot water heater, your roof, and security setup are all prone to wear out over time. Replacing them should not be a chance or a guess or seeking the best price available at the time. Instead, it should be a clearly defined system of replacement.

At some point in the life of your building, things begin to wear out, die, or break down.

When you replace any of these items, always try to select the same brand, make, and model. It makes replacing parts a lot easier. This includes everything from toilet seat covers to mini blinds.

There was a time when used appliances were much cheaper than brand new ones. That is no longer the case. With so many big box retailers now in the appliance business, prices have dropped dramatically.

If you need an item and you're a risk taker, you might explore eBay or Amazon for your purchase.

I had several older buildings and there were shops in town that specialized in antique furnishings, light fixtures, etc. Many of my residents LOVED the fact that their unit had these older fixtures because they felt it added real charm to their homes.

Preventative maintenance
Here is a list of items you must maintain for safety and security reasons.
1. Outdoor lighting
2. Furnace system
3. Water heater
4. Roof
5. Locks on all doors for the building proper or individual units
6. Indoor lighting in all common areas

Going green for energy savings
There is a growing awareness that energy conservation will increasingly have a direct impact on the valuations of real estate properties worldwide. It's already happening around the country and in whatever market you may be perusing right now.

Major REITs and real estate developers now routinely add energy and water usage as an important equation into the overall costs of development and maintenance of properties in all categories. Global players such Siemens now routinely include sustainability in every design project they take on. One industry study showed a 20 percent reduction in water usage by the use of restrictors on showerheads and faucets alone. Your properties should be no different.

It was not only the increased awareness of environmental issues and new government mandates that spurred this realization among industry officials. Most financial projections for real estate showed the price of energy and water escalating well ahead of the overall inflation rate. The U.S. demand for electricity alone is projected to rise at least 30% over the next thirty years.

In addition, local municipalities are increasingly tightening up energy usage standards for commercial and multi-family properties. Therefore, the control of those energy costs would have a direct impact on their bottom line and thus a competitive differentiator.

Aside from reducing their carbon footprint, lowering energy costs and enhancing sustainability; owners also realized that there was a changing mindset among their customers. Buyers, residents, residents, and investors were all coming to expect this kind of action. Being green and planning for sustainability is increasingly being seen as the right thing to do and has evolved into the right way of doing business. It directly affects your environmental, economic, and social impact on your neighborhood, your city, and the world.

The first step for a first time buyer would be to focus on the 'low hanging fruit.' In other words, concentrate on those areas where you can make the easiest and quickest impact on your energy costs. This is as true with your own home as it is with any real estate property you might own. The basic energy savings principles apply no matter what kind of property is involved.

You could begin by installing low-flow fixtures in all your showers and faucets throughout each unit. Whenever it came time for me to replace an appliance, I always bought the most energy efficient stove or refrigerator I could find. With large big box retailers such as Best Buy now selling appliances, there is healthy competition and good prices if you take the time to search them out.

Upon purchasing any building, I immediately replaced all the light bulbs within each unit and in all public areas with energy efficient light bulbs or lighting fixtures. My outside lights were either on a timer or had motion sensors.

Energy efficient lighting, low-flow fixtures and energy efficient appliances all have the shortest payback time in terms of cost savings. There are also other areas just as easy to upgrade and reducing your energy usage at minimum cost.

You don't need the 'blower door' diagnostic test to measure just how tight your doors and windows are. A cold draft can chill any room even if the furnace is operating at peak efficiency. Use your open palm or a piece of paper to measure just how strong the drafts are coming in from doors and windows. Don't forget to test the areas around heating and air conditioning ducts and vents. Basement windows are notorious for strong drafts that in turn will cool your basement during the winter months.

I made it an annual summer project to reseal and chalk all of my outside windows and doors each year. In the fall, I offered clear sheets of plastic to those residents who wanted to seal up the windows in their sunroom. Most accepted the offer and were very happy to take a few minutes to stop the pesky drafts from cooling that area. I also encouraged them to report to me any other areas in their units they felt were cool so that I could address those issues too.

In that same light, don't forget to feel your pipes in the basement. Any pipe that carries hot water should be insulated so that heat isn't lost in its transfer upstairs. Simple foam insulators are cheap and easy to install. While their impact may be minimal, their overall effectiveness over time will add up.

In addition to upgrading appliances within each unit, I also had my boilers, both steam and hot water, tuned up each fall. When it came time to replace my water heaters, I examined just how much water I would need for my units and purchased accordingly. Most of the water heaters I removed had been oversized for the amount of water needed per building. The new ones were more energy efficient, properly sized for the volume of water needed, and much cheaper to operate.

One of the first actions I took when purchasing a building was to access the location of the buildings thermostat and move it if necessary. Since these were older buildings, the thermostat was often in one of the units. More often than not, it was in a unit that had been occupied for years by a single resident or couple. They were used to controlling the heat and liked it that way.

The trick is to take that action right up front when you come in as the new owner. The residents have no idea what to expect and establishing firm guidelines for energy usage is extremely important to get your message across that you are serious about energy conservation.

If I couldn't move a thermostat because of the costs of doing so then I always placed a plastic shield over the unit and made sure it couldn't be tampered with by the resident.

I explained that if their unit was comfortable, then the others units would be too. They usually accepted that explanation and understood my actions.

Think Before You Act

In my zest to get one thermostat out of a unit occupied by an elderly couple who thought nothing of cranking it up to 85 degrees in the Fall, I moved the thermostat to the basement. Big mistake!

The basement was the coldest part of the building in the first place. Then every time a resident came through the front door, it created a draft that rushed downstairs chilling the area even more.

Temperatures began to fluctuate throughout the building and individual units. Residents complained about the inconsistency. When I talked to the installer they recommended a separate heater in the front lobby which I could only see as more problematic than helpful.

I finally had to move the thermostat back into one of the units and cover it with a protective plate. It was a costly exercise for me that could have been prevented if I had talked to other building owners or analyzed its placement in the first place.

Overall, energy conservation and sustainability is a systematic process. You should take both a long-term and a short-term approach to each building. As I mentioned before, you should initially take the quick actions that can bring immediate results. Then focus on longer term projects.

Near the end of my tenure as an apartment owner, I was researching the viability of high-energy heat pumps, smart metering, high efficiency tankless water heaters, combi-boilers, on-off lighting systems, LEED certification, and finally the application of apps to help me manage my properties. I was interested in anything and everything that might help me with all kinds of energy savings, sustainability, and making each property more energy efficient.

Start by doing everything you can easily accomplish to cut costs. Then, as appliances need to be replaced make sure you are getting the most cost and energy effective product you can buy. Make sure furnaces are always operating at their peak efficiency and make sure to control the thermostat yourself and not leave it up to one of the residents.

Plan for the long-term in which investments today may take months or years to see significant results. Either action is better than no action at all.

By making your buildings more energy efficient, you will not only add to your bottom-line savings, you will have a product that is more attractive to potential renters and any future buyer.

New technologies
Most new apartment owners are clueless about technology. Unfortunately, that is no longer acceptable in today's world

of increasing energy costs and more stringent state and federal energy saving requirements. If you can envision your apartment building as home to a number of residents who deserve the same comfort and convenience as a single homeowner, then it simply makes a lot of sense to know what technologies might help you in that area...as well as provide savings to your bottom line.

'Smart' (as in technology-enhanced) buildings save money and energy resources. They have monitoring systems/solutions in place that give building owners immediate notification relative to security, maintenance, and emergency issues. Smart buildings notify owners when something is amiss before human senses are able to detect or discover the problem. Any building owner will tell you that it is far easier and cheaper to fix a problem when it is small verses afterwards when it has grown in volume or severity.

Every day media outlets carry stories of new products and developments all designed for sustainability design.

A NEST thermostat is a new kind of animal. Simply stated, it analyzes user behavior to minimize energy usage. The heart of this beast is a wide array of sensors and artificial intelligence algorithms that capitalize on user behavior in ways no one thought possible just a few short years ago.

A second new device has been released. It's a new version of the old reliable smoke detector. Again, while the new device performs like any other smoke alarm, it takes its role and function a lot farther than any others on the market today.

Just like the NEST thermostat, this new device will track its users and subtly influence their behaviors. This new kind of smoke detector can distinguish between smoke and steam. Internet connectivity will direct its user to where the danger lies. A calculated and calm tone of voice will issue directions and warm lighting will guide owners if the lights all go out.

With rare exception, household appliances haven't changed much since the days of black and white television. But as these two new NEST products highlight, that old world is evolving at a rapid pace.

Another new product is an app created by SmartThings.com which describes itself as one seriously smart app. This app can coordinate many different functions in the home from monitoring energy output to security functions.

The world as we once knew it is changing and quickly becoming a programmable world. In our homes, automobiles, workplaces and entertainment spots, we're constantly surrounded by tiny intelligent sensors that are constantly capturing data about how we live and what we do on a daily basis. Many of these devices are now talking to one another and offering unheard of opportunities in managing properties.

Already in many commercial buildings, wireless networks monitor and maintain HVAC systems, alarm systems, internal technology usage, energy usage, the movement of air, and a host of other operational functions. These technology systems are gradually making their way into multi-family properties as well.

In the near future, the intelligence once locked tightly in our everyday devices and appliances will be unlocked and able to flow seamlessly into and through this new world of programming objects. Some have called it the Internet of Things or the Internet of Everything or the Industrial Internet or simply the Sensor Revolution. No matter its moniker, it will mean that these devices are no longer simply sources of data but instead they will become one coherent system.

Once this stage is reached, it will be possible to create a bona fide platform that can run software in much the same manner that a computer or smartphone can. That being said, we will be able to create an environment for each building we own that will take over many of the duties now being performed by the owner or maintenance person.

This new world will change the way we think about the division between our virtual world and our physical one. We will be able to automate activities we would normally do by hand and use intelligence from the cloud to monitor and maintain our facilities there.

These products from Smart Things and NEST are just the proverbial tip of the iceberg. There will be an avalanche of new products and services flooding the marketplace in the near future. While many initial applications will be aimed at the residential home market, their usage will spill over to multi-family and commercial buildings. It will only be a matter of time before apartment buildings, large and small, will have to join the growing list of intelligent buildings.

Management companies
In the real world of managing properties, you do not make money by paying someone to do the work you can do yourself. There are exceptions such as critical repairs, some electrical and plumbing work, and other service work that required professional expertise. Realistically, if it is something you can do, then do it and don't pay someone else.

You can't win with a management company. The only time I've found that a management company was advantageous was with out of state properties. I once had a condominium lose its air conditioning on the Fourth of July in southern California. Luckily for me, the management company took care of the problem...at a great expense to me - but at least the issue was resolved relatively quickly.

If you live in the same city as your rental properties, it is much cheaper to handle the property yourself vs. using a management company. Over the long run, it will be substantially cheaper to handle issues yourself than to let them do it for you.

Not all 'repairs' are a good idea
Even before the advent of Do-It-Yourself Television and the false idea that any change is an improvement to the property, I made a number of well intentioned, sincere efforts at improving my property or units. In many instances, it was a total waste of time and money.

I've already talked about my small debacle when I switched the thermostat from a unit to the basement and then had to move it up into another unit again.

One time I thought I would brighten up a kitchen so I wallpapered the walls with (what I thought) was an attractive and lively pattern. The new resident almost immediately asked if she could tear it off and repaint the walls herself (she hated it that much!).

I thought I'd paint a newly vacant unit with a tan color instead of plain old boring white. Guess what... no more than three months into their lease, the occupants begged to be able to paint their walls white again.

At first, I used to hang plastic in the sunrooms of one of my buildings because of a draft in almost all of the units. I would always knock and knock before I entered their unit. The residents seemed to appreciate my eliminating their draft and since they could still see out those sunroom windows having the plastic sheets there wasn't a bother. I always left a note on the door of each unit when I intended to hang the plastic unless I was told otherwise by the occupant.

One time my son and I knocked and knocked then entered one unit. It seemed empty so we promptly began to hang the plastic. Suddenly out walked one of the renters in her housecoat (I couldn't even see her ankles). She was scared and screamed at us to leave.

She wrote me an angry letter denouncing me for sneaking into her apartment as she lay sleeping in her bed. She threatened to sue me if I ever did that again. After that incident, I instead told my residents about the plastic sheets being available for free if THEY wanted to hang their own sheets. I never entered a unit 'unannounced' after that.

There were some other things I tried like motivational signs in the lobby (boring…no one noticed), plastic flowers on the front steps, (most of them got ripped off by bored neighborhood teens) and paintings in the laundry room. (Again, no one noticed or seemed to care.)

It seemed to be a never-ending quest on my part to find new ways to liven up or make the building more home-like. Some of them worked and others didn't. But I never stopped trying.

Laws, codes, and permits
It is your moral and legal obligation to provide a safe and secure home for your residents.

It is also essential if you are to avoid problems in the future. After that, it is up to each one of your residents to continue that process.

You must know and understand city, county, state, and federal guidelines in dealing with your residents. Moreover, always remember that the law is NOT on your side. In almost every instance, the laws are meant to protect the tenant, not the landlord. So understand your rights and the rights of your residents.

Safety rules to follow
These may sound obvious. However, surprisingly, these are not obvious to some residents - make sure you put these in writing in the lease, as well as in sign-form within the building(s).

No smoking inside, no grills inside, no open candles inside, and beware of Christmas trees. No gas cans inside the premises.

These are all NON-NEGOTIABLE and can be a reason for violating the lease. When it came to fire code violations or anything else that might endanger the lives of my residents, the issue was non-negotiable as far as I was concerned.

Rental codes
The twin cities of Minneapolis and Saint Paul have a stringent certificate of occupancy inspection program for rental units. It's really a mixed blessing for property owners.

In a perfect world, one wouldn't need a city inspector to tell him how to manage and maintain his property. This is not a perfect world and there are enough jerk landlords out there that this program is sorely needed.

Sadly, the program can be an enormous problem for the good landlords as well. Since you can't fight city hall the answer is to learn to shut up and play the game. For over thirty years, I had an average of one inspection for one of my buildings once a year. Understand that you can't win this game unless you play by their rules.

Inspections

First, be as prepared as you possibly can because you will have to fix something. I have NEVER met a code inspector who passed my properties on first inspection.

The inspector will not, cannot, just pass your property on the first visit. It just won't happen! The best way to compete in this game is to keep your building and its units up to code just as a matter of habit. It's much easier to make repairs and deal with small issues as they arise rather than a major issue that the first inspector is certain to find at some point. So learn to do it right the first time.

St. Paul finally got it right. After years of punishing good property owners, the city got smart and decided to create different classifications instead of just throwing the good property owners in with the bad ones. There were still inspections but once a good landlord passed inspection, there wasn't another one for several years. It came too late for my real estate career, but might be helpful for you in yours.

Chapter Summary:

Attention to basic maintenance issues and upkeep of facilities mean fewer problems down the line and a better ROI. It also means more satisfied residents. There are a growing number of new technologies to help cut costs and enhance sustainability.

YOUR FUTURE PROSPERITY AND GROWTH

You will be able to predict your monthly cash flow while at the same time building equity in your property. Over time, your building will probably appreciate in value without any effort on your part. There are also numerous tax benefits for you as a property owner.

Then you will learn how to leverage those assets to continue to grow your business. In addition, you will learn how to add value to your buildings while keeping your residents in place. You will learn that the little things can make a big difference in your bottom line. Over time, you can compound your success in one building and transfer that success to every other building you own or buy.

Build a business and still have a life
As I mentioned at the beginning of this guide, it is not meant to be the absolute answer for every question about managing small apartment buildings. Everyone's background is different and what you bring to the table in terms of a willingness to work hard and focus on these suggestions will directly affect your outcome.

It is a beginning. This guide will start you out on the path to financial prosperity and, if you so choose, a lifelong career in real estate. It can also help you establish a business that can, to a great degree, run itself. It can provide an ancillary income stream to your other financial or career endeavors.

Use your equity to expand your real estate portfolio

If you have built a business model that is producing a positive cash flow then you can use that equity to expand your business. You may choose to buy more apartment buildings or expand into other areas of real estate. The principles espoused here can be applied to one or one hundred apartment buildings. Residents are the same the world over. Treat them well and they will return the favor.

Be on the cutting edge of new developments in real estate

Part of your success in this business will depend on your ability to be aware of and a part of the cutting edge of new technologies. Many new technologies can help you manage your properties and stay focused on time management as you begin to add more properties to your growing portfolio.

A personal suggestion ... do not tell people you're a landlord.

It was always one of my pet peeves. One, I might add, that my family did not necessarily agree with but they humored me anyway. We never talked about 'the buildings' outside of home and never in front of other people.

I owned apartment buildings for thirty plus years and no one knew about them except my kids, the taxman, and our financial planner. No one else knew because there was never a 'need to know' on anyone else's part. I learned very quickly about the numerous misconceptions around property ownership - especially rental property.

While labeling yourself as a landlord or a property owner might be a nice boost to your ego, it is inherently misleading and simply sets you up for all kinds of trouble. If people find out you own real estate, they tend to immediately assume:

- You must be rich to have other properties aside from your home.
- You must have deep pockets and thus would be a likely target for other investments.
- You must be making a killing on the rents and appreciation.
- You're a slumlord.
- You're a real life Donald Trump and they want your advice - or worse, your money.

Who needs the hassle or that kind of attitude from others? I never asked my friends about their investments, salary, or net worth. In turn, they had no reason to know mine.

Create a lifestyle that best suits your personality
Lastly and most importantly, this guide will allow you to create a lifestyle that best suits your personality. You can determine just how much time you want to spend on your real estate portfolio while still being engaged in other aspects of your life.

It still means a lot of hard work at first or at times when issues arise. Overall, following these guidelines will allow you to let most of your buildings and their residents manage themselves. With an attention to detail and the willingness to work steadily toward your financial goal and aspirations, you can succeed beyond anything you can imagine today.

GLOSSARY OF REAL ESTATE TERMS

Appraisals: This is just one of several steps to determine a fair value for the property you may want to buy. It is a valuation of property (ie. real estate, a business, an antique) by the estimate of an authorized person. This can sometimes be a tricky proposition and a second appraisal may be desired. In order to be a valid appraisal, the authorized person will have a designation from a regulatory body governing the jurisdiction the appraiser operates within.

Appreciation: This is one of the prime benefits of owning real estate. While never a guarantee, a rise in property values is one of the main reasons people invest in real estate. Simply stated, appreciation is an increase in the value of an asset over time. The increase can occur for a number of reasons including increased demand or weakening supply, or as a result of changes in inflation or interest rates. This is the opposite of depreciation, which is a decrease over time.

Building Codes: Every city, county and state is different in their approach to building codes. It is imperative that you know and understand those particular rules and regulations that might affect your property. On face value, building codes are simply a series of ordinances enacted by a state or local governmental entity, establishing minimum requirements that must be met in the construction and maintenance of buildings. Here is a good example of the phrase: 'knowledge is power.'

Building Permits: This is a type of authorization that must be granted by a government or other regulatory body before the construction of a new or existing *building* can legally occur. It is always good to know the rules here even if you have no immediate plans to make changes to your properties.

Cash Flow: Positive cash flow should be your goal with any property you own. It is defined as the total amount of money being transferred into and out of a business, especially as affecting liquidity.

Certificate of Occupancy: This is a document issued by a local government agency or building department certifying a building's compliance with applicable building codes and other laws, and indicating it to be in a condition suitable for occupancy. It is paramount that you know and understand the guidelines behind your city's Certificate of Occupancy standards.

Comps: Real estate recently sold nearby that is similar in size/value - 'comparable' - to the property you are looking at purchasing. Comps are used as part of a formula by real property appraisers to calculate the value of a property for sale.

Contract for Deed: Oftentimes this is the most attractive means by which to purchase your properties. A Contract for Deed is a contract between a seller and buyer of real property in which the seller provides financing to the buyer to purchase the property for an agreed-upon purchase price and the buyer repays the loan in installments.

It is imperative that you understand the legalities of a Contract for Deed because you 'don't really own' your property until that Contract is fully paid off.

Craigslist: The website www.craigslist.org is a site where buyers, sellers, and renters can post and view ads - usually for free. Although it has gotten a bad rap in the past for some of its ads, Craigslist is still a good way to attract residents providing you take the proper safeguards when you do your advertising.

Credit Report: There are pros and cons to using a credit report in selecting residents. While it is true that a credit report is a detailed report of an individual's credit history prepared by a credit bureau and used by a lender to in determining a loan applicant's creditworthiness there are many other factors that must go into your selection process.

Curb Appeal: I cannot emphasize enough the importance of having a visually attractive look to your property. On one level curb appeal is simply the visual attractiveness of the exterior of a residential or commercial property, as viewed from the street. It is used as an indicator of the initial appeal of a property to prospective buyers. But more importantly, it sends a message to anyone passing by that this is a well-maintained building and a good place to live.

Discounted Paper: Some real estate investors only deal with these securities that are issued at a discount and mature at face, or par value. The difference, rather than coupon payments, represents the interest earned at maturity.

Earned Income: This is defined as money obtained from paid work. Some folks see it as the opposite of appreciation in which you are gaining equity in your building without hard labor to do it.

Earnest Money: This is defined as a deposit showing the seller that a buyer is serious about purchasing a property.

When the transaction is finalized, the funds are put toward the buyer's down payment. If the deal falls through, the buyer may not be able to reclaim the deposit.

Energy Audit: In todays world of ever-rising energy costs it is imperative that you understand just what your energy usage is for each one of your properties. This assessment of the energy needs and efficiency of a building or buildings will help you plan for energy savings in the future..

Equity: This can be a tricky concept to understand but it important to understand for success in real estate investing. Equity is defined as the residual value or interest of the most junior class of investors in assets, after all liabilities are paid; if liability exceeds assets, negative *equity* exists.

Fiduciary Responsibility: It is necessary to know and understand your rights and responsibilities as an apartment owner. Fiduciary responsibility is defined as a legal duty to act solely in another party's interests. Parties owing this duty are called fiduciaries. The individuals to whom they owe a duty are called principals.

Fixer-Upper: Most of us think of this as a house in need of repairs but, in fact, it could also describe an apartment building in need of major or minor repairs to increase its value and attractiveness to new residents.

Flipping Properties: This real estate strategy comes and goes in and out of flavor depending on the current economy. In this approach to real estate investing, an investor purchases properties with the goal of reselling them for a profit. Profit is generated either through the price appreciation that occurs as a result of a hot housing market and/or from renovations and capital improvements.

Remember not all flips are profitable and most require

extensive knowledge of remodeling techniques and associated costs.

Foreclosure: This is the process of taking possession of a mortgaged property as a result of the mortgagor's failure to keep up mortgage payments.

Some real estate investment books suggest that foreclosures are the only way to go. Again, let the buyer beware. A foreclosure might provide a quick turn-around to profits or a legal quagmire that can tie up an investor for months or years.

Fractional Ownership: This is one of those 'in and out of flavor' investment schemes. It is a method in which several unrelated parties can share in, and mitigate the risk of ownership of a high-value tangible asset, usually a jet, yacht or piece of resort real estate. It can be done for strictly monetary reasons, but typically there is some amount of personal access involved.

Government Tax Liens: This is a last resort to force an individual or business to pay back taxes. To get rid of a lien, the taxpayer must pay what he or she owes, get the debt dismissed in bankruptcy court or reach an offer in compromise with the tax authorities.

Green Buildings: Although it was once seen as a temporary fad the idea of making buildings energy-efficient has proven to be both practical and profitable. Simply stated, this is the practice of creating structures and using processes that are environmentally responsible and resource-efficient throughout a building's life-cycle from siting to design, construction, operation, maintenance, renovation and deconstruction.

Gross Income: This is an individual's total personal income before taking taxes or deductions into account or a company's revenue minus cost of goods sold

Homesteading: Many investors don't know that small apartment buildings are perfect vehicles for homesteading. Homesteading is defined as property that is designated by a householder as the householder's home and protected by law from forced sale to meet debts.

HVAC: Acronym for 'Heating, Ventilation, and Air Conditioning'.

Interest Rates: This is the proportion of a loan that is charged as interest to the borrower, typically expressed as an annual percentage of the loan outstanding. It is imperative that you undertstand the impact your loan's interest rate might have on your bottom line in managing (and paying for) your apartment building.

LEED [Leadership in Energy and Environmental Design]: A set of rating systems for the design, construction, operation, and maintenance of green buildings, homes, and neighborhoods.

Leverage: This is the hallmark of good real estate investing. It is to use borrowed capital for (an investment), expecting the profits made to be greater than the interest payable.

LLC [Limited Liability Corporation]: A corporate structure whereby the members of the company cannot be held personally liable for the company's debts or liabilities

Low Income Housing: Don't let the title scare you away. A well-maintained and properly managed property can still be profitable. Low income housing is defined as any housing that is limited to occupancy by persons whose family income does not exceed certain preset maximum levels relating to poverty levels.

Mailbox money: This is one of the many promises that some real estate promoters promise other investors. It is money that supposedly comes from investments in which no participation is needed from the investor.

Market Value: The price an asset would fetch in the open and free marketplace.

MLS [Multiple Listing Service]: A marketing database set up by a group of cooperating real estate brokers.

Negative Cash Flow: Sometimes upon an initial investment in a property there can be a negative cash flow. This is defined as a situation where the cash outflows during a period are higher than the cash inflows during the same period.

While it may be acceptable upon the initial purchase, an investor should work very hard to correct that and create a positive cash flow as soon as possible.

Net Income: Total earnings (or profit). Net income is calculated by taking revenues and adjusting for the cost of doing business, depreciation, interest, taxes and other expenses.

Passive Income: This is one way of looking at your monthly rents. It could be thought of as passive **income** which is an **income** received on a regular basis, with little effort required to maintain it.

Positive Cash Flow: Situation where the cash inflows during a period are higher than the cash outflows during the same period.

Preventative Maintenance: This should be one of your top priorities in owning any property. It is defined as the care and servicing by personnel for the purpose of maintaining equipment and facilities in satisfactory operating condition by providing for systematic inspection, detection, and correction of incipient failures either before they occur or before they develop into major defects.

Property Management Firms: A simple definition is that these are companies hired to act in the best interests of the owner to maintain the property, keep it occupied with residents, collect rents, budget improvements and maintain records.

Like so many other aspects of owning rental property, let the buyer beware. Know exactly what you are getting into before you hand over management of your properties to someone else.

Property Manager: Some are very good. Others leave a lot to desire. A property manager is a person or firm charged with operating a real estate property for a fee, when the owner is unable to personally attend to such details, or is not interested in doing so.

The best guideline here is to thoroughly review their past history and check references to make sure the person you hire is best suited to manage your particular property.

REI [Real Estate Investment]: Acronym for 'Real Estate Investment(s)'

REIT [Real Estate Investment Trust]: This is another kind of real estate investment for some but totally different from actually managing your own properties. A REIT is a company that owns, and in most cases, operates income-producing real estate. REITs own many types of commercial real estate, ranging from office and apartment buildings to warehouses, hospitals, shopping centers, hotels and even timberlands.

Rental Application: Be sure to know and understand just what kind of information you can (legally) collect before presenting any rental application to a prospective resident. This document is used to collect information by landlords or apartment complexes so that the landlord may make a decision to accept or decline a prospective resident. Landlords will usually use information from the application to run a credit and criminal history report.

Rental History: This means different things to different property owners since most rental history reports go beyond just looking at your past as it relates to housing. Therefore, having a good rental history means more than just always paying your rent on time and may include a credit report, eviction report, criminal record search, record of payment timelines (did you pay on time).

ROI [Return on Investment]: There are several ways to determine ROI, but the most frequently used method is to divide net profit by total assets.

Section 8 / Section 55: The rules regulating this kind of housing can vary from state to state and city to city. On one level it is defined as any housing that is limited to occupancy by persons whose family income does not exceed certain preset maximum levels relating to poverty levels.

It is imperative that owners understand the legality of these voucher programs before accepting any resident who is on them.

Security Deposit: A sum of money held in trust either as an initial part-payment in a purchasing process - also known as an earnest payment, or else, in the course of a rental agreement to ensure the cost of repair in relation to any damage explicitly specified in the lease and that did in fact occur.

Seller Financing: This is how I financed my own buildings. It isn't always available or perhaps not the most attractive way to purchase a building. Simply stated it is a **loan** provided by the **seller** of a property or business to the purchaser. Usually, the purchaser will make some sort of down payment to the **seller**, and then make installment payments (usually on a monthly basis) over a specified time, at an agreed-upon interest rate, until the **loan** is fully repaid.

The type of financing is just one of many factors like interest rates that go into deciding what financial route to take in purchasing your building.

Straw Man Theory: Sales tactic by which one is led to believe that if you don't jump at the deal, there are others waiting in the wings to grab it from you or there is a better price already offered. (Don't believe it! They wouldn't be wasting their time with you if there was a concrete offer on the table.)

Teardowns: Property purchased that will simply be torn down to make way for a larger dwelling.

Time Share: The arrangement whereby several joint owners have the right to use a property as a vacation home under a time-sharing agreement.

Umbrella Coverage: Building owners get sued. That is a fact of life. I have always taken the position that it is better to be prepared than to be surprised down the road. Umbrella coverage is defined as liability **insurance** that is in excess of specified other **policies** and also potentially primary

insurance for losses not covered by the other **policies**.

Vacancy: Too many vacancies can kill cash flow and present headaches to building owners. Vacancy refers to something being unoccupied. If an apartment has vacancies, there are units available to rent.

Valuations: An estimation of something's worth, especially one carried out by a professional appraiser.

Value Add-Ons: This is one of the first things I would always look for in any property I was considering for purchase. It is the practice of finding anything that can either increase the product's price or value. For example, offering one year of free support on a new computer would be a value-added feature.

Value Investing: You might say this is another way of looking for properties can be improved upon so that their value increased over time more rapidly than it might do so otherwise. For savvy investors, it is the strategy of selecting investments that trade for less than their intrinsic values. Value investors actively seek stocks of companies that they believe the market has undervalued. They believe the market overreacts to good and bad news, resulting in stock price movements that do not correspond with the company's long-term fundamentals. The result is an opportunity for value investors to profit by buying when the price is deflated.

ABOUT THE AUTHOR

Upon leaving the service and graduating from college, Denis embarked on a career that was as varied as his life experiences. Like many entrepreneurs, Denis J. LaComb started multiple businesses through the years; and real estate particularly appealed to him.

It was during his thirty-plus years working fulltime in television, as well as managing his own video production/distribution business, that Denis became involved in real estate. Not just any real estate venture; but the purchase and management of small apartment buildings. With a full work load, his own thriving video business, and two small children demanding his time; Denis created a system that allowed him to operate his real estate business while working fulltime and still 'having a life.'

Starting with just one five-unit building, he built a thriving portfolio of properties that practically ran themselves. Denis developed a set of management techniques that helped him allocate his time and avoid so many of the mistakes other real estate investors make.

Denis has decided to share his experiences; successful and otherwise, with readers who might be interested in real estate investments. He has designed this apartment management guide to be realistic and practical with proven guidelines that greatly enhance the probability of success.

Denis hopes this guide will help propel its readers toward achieving great success and profitability in apartment investment and management … while still having a life.

Connect with Denis online

Official Website
www.DenisJLaComb.com

Facebook
www.facebook.com/denisjlacombofficial

Blog
denisjlacomb.blogspot.com

Twitter
@AuthorDLaComb

Other Titles by Denis J. LaComb
Apache Death Wind
Love in the A Shau
Apache Blue Eyes

Other Projects in Development by Denis J. LaComb
Debris Trilogy
Follow the Cobbler
Apache Death Wind Trilogy
Trans Con
Wake: The Musical
Sweet Pea & The Gang
Siloso

www.ingramcontent.com/pod-product-compliance
Lightning Source LLC
Chambersburg PA
CBHW051717170526
45167CB00002B/697